ESSENCE OF HINDUISM

SWAMI MUKUNDANANDA

Bal-Mukund Character Building Series

Radha Govind Dham
XVII/3305, Ranjit Nagar
New Delhi - 110008 India

Published by
Jagadguru Kripaluji Yog
7405 Stoney Point Dr
Plano, TX 75025 USA

www.jkyog.org

ISBN: 978-0-9826675-8-3

Illustrations: Sanjay Sarkar, Saurabh Pandey
Design and Composition: Graphics Spot

Jagadguru Shree Kripaluji Maharaj

DEDICATION

This book is dedicated to my Beloved Spiritual Master, Jagadguru Shree Kripaluji Maharaj, who is illuminating this world with the purest rays of Divine knowledge and love.

He has taught us by his example, the importance of nurturing souls with love and care, to help them realize a glorious future. He has given us the supreme process of building a noble value system by teaching selfless Divine love.

I am confident that by his blessings this book will be helpful in inspiring and elevating seekers, thereby creating a better world for all of us.

Swami Mukundananda

ABOUT THE AUTHOR

Swami Mukundananda is a world-renowned spiritual teacher from India, and is the senior disciple of Jagadguru Shree Kripaluji Maharaj. He is the founder of the Yogic system called "Jagadguru Kripaluji Yog."

Swamiji is a unique sanyāsī (in the renounced order of life), who has a distinguished technical and management educational background as well. He completed B.Tech. from the world-renowned Indian Institute of Technology (IIT), Delhi. He then did MBA from the equally distinguished Indian Institute of Management (IIM), Kolkata. After that, he worked for some time with one of India's topmost industrial houses.

However, distinguished material education and a promising corporate career did not quench his thirst for knowing the Absolute Truth. The longing for God was so strong that he renounced his career and travelled throughout India as a sanyāsī. During these travels, he got the opportunity to closely associate with many elevated Saints of India, read the writings of the great Āchāryas of the past, and reside in many famous holy places.

Ultimately his search took him to the lotus feet of his Spiritual Master, Jagadguru Shree Kripaluji Maharaj (who is lovingly called "Maharajji" by his devotees). He was overawed by the unfathomable scriptural knowledge and ocean of Divine Love that he saw manifest in his Spiritual Master. About this first meeting, Maharajji later remarked, "He recognized me as one would recognize his mother."

Under the guidance of Shree Maharajji, he practiced intense sādhanā while residing at the āśhram. He also extensively studied the Vedic scriptures, and the Indian and Western systems of philosophy.

Upon completion of his studies, his Guru entrusted him with the key task of propagating the ancient knowledge of the Eternal Truth the world over.

For the last quarter of a century, Shree Swamiji has been traveling far and wide, awakening hundreds of thousands of seekers. Wherever Swamiji goes, he attracts huge audiences. Hearing the profound secrets of the Vedas from him is a rare privilege, for he is able to explain the ancient esoteric knowledge with rigourous scientific logic, in the modern context. Using perfect logic, and a simple-yet-scientific approach, Swamiji offers new ways of understanding and applying the knowledge of the scriptures in our daily lives. The hallmark of his lectures is the ease with which he dispels various myths and misnomers associated with the various paths of God-realization, and his ability to penetrate even the toughest minds and convince them with depth of understanding and scriptural veracity.

Swamiji's lectures cover the teachings of the Vedas, Upanishads, Shreemad Bhagavatam, Purānas, Bhagavad Geeta, Ramayan, and other Eastern scriptures and Western philosophies. Like the true Disciple of a true Master, Swamiji masterfully quotes from the scriptures of all the great religions, to satisfy even the most discerning of knowledge-seekers. He also reveals the simple and straightforward path to God-realization that can be practiced by anyone.

Although Swamiji started preaching in India two decades ago, he now preaches both in India and abroad. He has inspired innumerable devotees in Singapore, Malaysia, and Hong Kong, where his visit is always anxiously awaited. Since 2008, on the instruction of Shree Maharajji, Swamiji has increasingly begun spending more time in USA, where his educational background and command over the English language make his programs particularly charming to the intelligentsia, professionals, and academicians.

Shree Swamiji has founded many organizations in India with permanent centers and āśhrams, such as Jagadguru Kripaluji Yog Trust, India, Radha Govind Dham in Delhi, Radha Krishna Bhakti Mandir in Cuttack, Radha Govind Dham in Berhampur, Shyama Shyam Dham in Jajpur, Radha Govind Dham in Parla Khemundi, Radha Govind Dham in Karanjia, etc. In USA, Swamiji has inspired the formation of Jagadguru Kripaluji Yog, a 501(c)(3) non-profit organization. In the space of a few years, JKYog centers have opened throughout the length and breadth of USA.

Swamiji cares deeply about imparting Hindu cultural and religious values to the younger generation, especially in the West. Towards this end, he has conceived a special Personality Development program for children and young adults. This program is called "The Bal-Mukund Playground for Vedic Wisdom." It includes character building, yog, meditation, devotional singing, and religious training. Many Bal-Mukund centers have been started for the benefit of children, both in USA and India.

Shree Swamiji has a God-gifted ability to keep all kinds of audiences enthralled and entertained through wisdom filled anecdotes, humorous stories and irrefutable logic. He has inspired innumerable people, of all ages, towards the path of God Realization, the world over. Swamiji's warmth and humility touch all those who have the fortune to have his association. In fact, his very presence radiates Grace and Bliss.

- The Editor

FOREWORD

The human form that we all have received is a tremendous opportunity provided by God to know the Absolute Truth, and to attain the perfection that our soul has been seeking since eternity. This highest goal requires the highest knowledge for its accomplishment. That pure and divine knowledge is the most powerful thing in this world, and people who get access to such uplifting knowledge receive the key to elevating their lives to sublime heights.

The Vedic scriptures are a vast treasure-house of the most resplendent divine knowledge which contains the key for bringing a divine transformation in our lives. Intuitively, seekers worldwide perceive that the heritage of India, the land of spirituality, holds in its bosom the rarest of rare secrets that they all yearn to know. That is why an inherent curiosity exists for understanding the concepts of Hinduism, reading its scriptures, and visiting the country that is the spiritual leader of the world.

However, without proper guidance, such endeavours to fathom the secrets of Hinduism, even with the best of intentions, do not meet with success. People get stumped with how to access the knowledge, comprehend its wide-spectrum of concepts and utilize them meaningfully in their lives. That is why Hinduism is an enigma for most westerners. Their clichéd understandings of Hinduism as a way of life etc. cannot fathom the precious treasure of gems in its repository.

Interestingly, Hinduism is not mentioned by that name anywhere in the Vedic scriptures. The word "Hindu" was first coined by the Arabs to refer to the people who lived on the other side of the river Indus (called Sindhu in Sanskrit). This gave rise to the word "Al-Hind" for the land across the river Indus, and the name of the religion they practiced became adopted in English as "Hinduism."

The Vedas, in contrast, have a very different and majestic perspective on the nomenclature of the religion that they teach. Since the Vedas are the eternal knowledge of God, the name of the religion described in them is called Sanātan Dharm, or "Eternal religion," It is the path to God-realization, based on scientific, non-sectarian, and eternal principles.

This book has been written with the goal of teaching those perennial principles of Sanātan Dharm, or the Eternal religion. Hence, the important teachings of all the Vedic scriptures are covered in this one book. The subject matter is presented in a manner that would make it comprehensible to everyone, including westerners and youth. At the same time, each concept is treated with philosophic depth for the satisfaction of the more learned and erudite readers. Along with quoting the important verses from the scriptures, practical examples from all walks of life have been used to demonstrate their relevance to everyday living.

The topics have been sequentially arranged to enable readers to reconcile the subject matter of all the Hindu scriptures in one place. They are based on the Philosophy of Divine Love, as presented by the Supreme Acharya of the present age, Jagadguru Shree Kripaluji Maharaj. Since the chapters follow a logical flow, it is recommended that the chapters be read in the same sequence. I sincerely pray that the "Essence of Hinduism" will illumine your intellect, move your heart, and nourish your soul, as you repeatedly turn to it for the spiritual succor that it contains.

Swami Mukundananda

Guide to Hindi Pronunciation

अ	*a*	as *u* in b*u*t
आ	*ā*	as *a* in f*a*r
इ	*i*	as *i* in p*i*n
ई	*ī*	as *i* in mach*i*ne
उ	*u*	as *u* in p*u*sh
ऊ	*ū*	as *o* in m*o*ve
ए	*e*	as *a* in ev*a*de
ऐ	*ai*	As *a* in mat; sometimes as *ai* in *ai*sle with the only difference that a should be pronounced as *u* in b*u*t, not as *a* in f*a*r.
ओ	*o*	as *o* in g*o*
औ	*au*	as *o* in pot, or as *aw* in *Saw*
ऋ	*ṛi*	as *r* in *Kṛiṣhṇa*
:	*ḥ*	it is a strong aspirate; also lengthens the preceding vowel and occurs only at the end of a word. It is pronounced as a final *h* sound
ं	*ṁ*	nasalizes and lengthens the preceding vowel and is pronounced as *n* in the French word Bon
क	*ka*	as *k* in kite
ख	*kha*	as *kha* in Eckhart
ग	*ga*	as *g* in goat
घ	*gha*	as *gh* in Dig hard

ङ	*ṅa*	as *n* in finger
च	*cha*	as *cha* in chair
छ	*chha*	as *chh* in staunch heart
ज	*ja*	as *j* in jar
झ	*jha*	as *dgeh* in Hedgehog
ञ	*ña*	as *n* in lunch
ट	*ṭa*	as *t* in tub
ठ	*ṭha*	as *th* in hothead
ड	*ḍa*	as *d* in divine
ढ	*ḍha*	as *dh* in Redhead
ण	*ṇa*	as *n* in burnt
त	*ta*	as *t* in French word matron
थ	*tha*	as *th* in ether
द	*da*	as *th* in either
ध	*dha*	as *dh* in Buddha
न	*na*	as *n* in no
प	*pa*	as *p* in pink
फ	*pha*	as *ph* in Uphill
ब	*ba*	as *b* in boy
भ	*bha*	as *bh* in abhor
म	*ma*	as *m* in man
य	*ya*	as *y* in yes
र	*ra*	as *r* in remember

ल	*la*	as *l* in light
व	*va*	as *v* in vine, as *w* in swan
श	*śha*	as *sh* in shape
स	*sa*	as *s* in sin
ष	*ṣha*	as *sh* in show
ह	*ha*	as *h* in hut
क्ष	*kṣha*	as *ksh* in freak show
ज्ञ	*gya*	as *gy* in big young
ड़	*ṛa*	There is no sign in English to represent the sounds ड़ and ढ़. They have been written as *ṛa* and *ṛha*, but the tip of the tongue quickly flaps down.

Table of Contents

Chapter 1 Nature of the Self

"I am reading." "I am eating." "I am walking." The awareness of "I" remains with us at all times. However, what is this "I"? This question has captured the interest of innumerable profound thinkers throughout history.

When you look at your family album, you find the picture of a newborn baby, and you say, "That is me." Then you see the

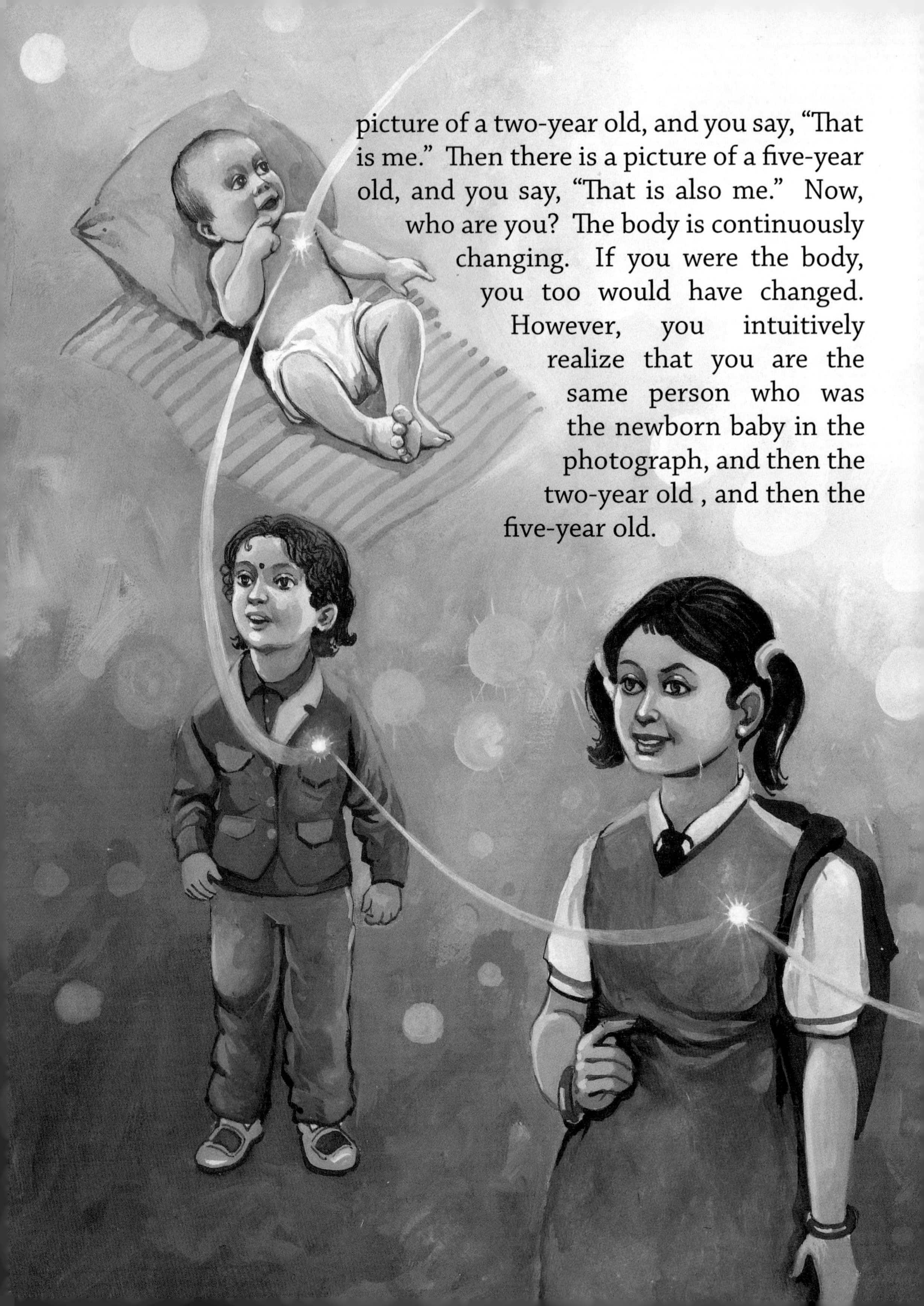

picture of a two-year old, and you say, "That is me." Then there is a picture of a five-year old, and you say, "That is also me." Now, who are you? The body is continuously changing. If you were the body, you too would have changed. However, you intuitively realize that you are the same person who was the newborn baby in the photograph, and then the two-year old , and then the five-year old.

From Science, we come to know that the body consists of trillions of cells. These cells keep dying and others are created in their place. The process of regeneration changes the whole body within a period of seven years. Yet, one remains the same person, despite constant change of the body. The Vedas teach us that within the body is the unchanging *ātmā*, or soul. That is the real "I", the real self. The body is material, while the *ātmā* is spiritual and immortal, like God.

The Evidence of the Soul – Consciousness

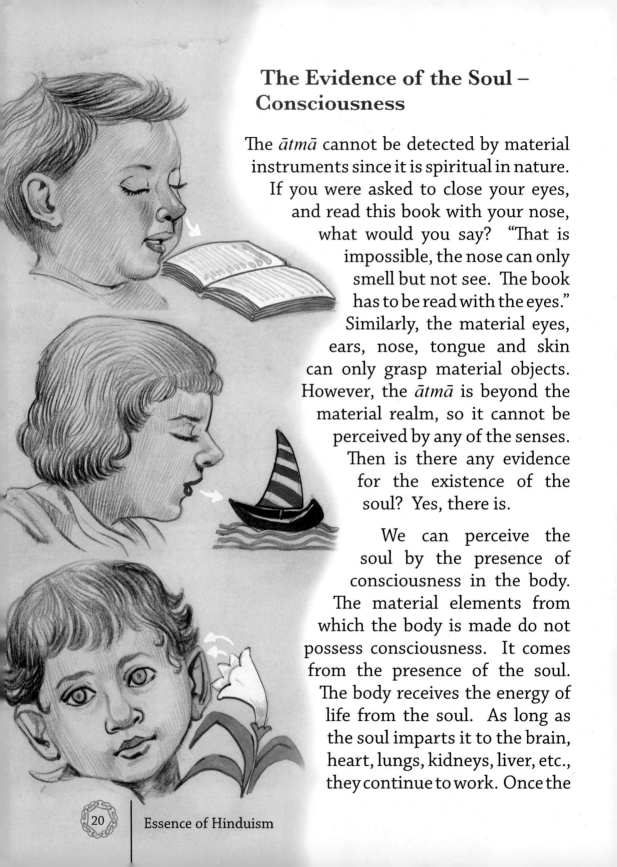

The *ātmā* cannot be detected by material instruments since it is spiritual in nature. If you were asked to close your eyes, and read this book with your nose, what would you say? "That is impossible, the nose can only smell but not see. The book has to be read with the eyes." Similarly, the material eyes, ears, nose, tongue and skin can only grasp material objects. However, the *ātmā* is beyond the material realm, so it cannot be perceived by any of the senses. Then is there any evidence for the existence of the soul? Yes, there is.

We can perceive the soul by the presence of consciousness in the body. The material elements from which the body is made do not possess consciousness. It comes from the presence of the soul. The body receives the energy of life from the soul. As long as the soul imparts it to the brain, heart, lungs, kidneys, liver, etc., they continue to work. Once the soul leaves, the organs and parts of the body are still there, but all work ceases. The body is now declared as dead. Hence, the symptom of the soul is life, or consciousness.

This consciousness does not exist in matter. Nor can it be created in the laboratory. Scientists can manipulate matter to create different forms. However, they cannot make matter conscious. Matter is thus termed "insentient", or lifeless, while all living creatures are termed "sentient", or possessing life. Consciousness is thus the evidence of the soul.

Size and Location of the Soul

The soul is extremely tiny and is seated in the region of the heart. The Vedas state:

हृदि ह्येष आत्मा। (प्रश्नोपनिषद् ३.६)

hṛidi hyeṣha ātmā (Praśhopaniṣhad 3.6)

"The soul is situated in the heart." Yet, it is not locked to the heart. During a heart-transplant, the soul would continue to reside in the heart region, even if the heart were removed and replaced.

Although it is situated in one place, the soul spreads its consciousness throughout the body. This is just as a light-bulb remains in one place, while its light spreads throughout the room. The soul too, while being seated in the heart, enlivens the entire body.

Immortality of the Soul

What we term as "death" is merely the soul changing bodies. For the soul, there is neither birth nor death. There was never a time when it did not exist, nor will there ever be a time when it will cease to be. The Vedic scriptures state:

वासांसि जीर्णानि यथा विहाय नवानि गृह्णाति नरोऽपराणि।
तथा शरीराणि विहाय जीर्णान्यन्यानि संयाति नवानि देही।।
(भगवद् गीता २.२२)

vāsānsi jīrṇāni yathā vihāya navāni gṛihṇāti naro 'parāṇi
tathā śharīrāṇi vihāya jīrṇānyanyāni sanyāti navāni dehī
(Bhagavad Geeta 2.22)

As a man sheds worn-out garments and wears new ones, likewise (at the time of death), the soul casts off its worn-out body and enters into a new one. The body is like a cloth for the *ātmā*. Every morning, you take off your old clothes and put on new ones. Similarly, when the body becomes unfit for the *ātmā* to reside in any longer, the soul leaves the body. It is then given a new body in accordance with its karmas. This process of giving up the old body is looked upon as "death," and the process of taking on a new body is called "birth."

In many cultures, the distinction between the soul and body is not clear. Thus, upon someone's death, they bury the body and assume that the person is lying in the grave. However, the soul is not in the grave; it has left for its destination to another body. What is buried in the grave will soon be eaten by worms and turn into mud. Thus, in the Indian tradition, the body is not buried after death. It is burnt, and prayers are offered for the departed soul.

Destination of the Soul after Death

God is All-knowing, and He always resides with the soul. He keeps an account of all the karmas of the soul, and gives the results. Upon death, God makes the soul take birth in another place in accordance with its karmas. There are 8.4 million life forms. The soul could be born in any of these species of life.

Amongst these life forms, the human life is special because it possesses the power of knowledge. With this special faculty, we humans also have a greater responsibility. For example, a Bank Manager is given a special room by the bank, while the cashier sits at the counter. However, the Bank Manager is also expected to fulfill a bigger responsibility. If the Manager decides to do only as much work as the cashier, the Bank will naturally withdraw the special room and ask the Manager to sit at the counter as well.

Similarly, God has especially given human beings the faculty of knowledge. He expects us to use this power to understand the Absolute Truth and attain it. Instead, if we make our goal to eat good foods, then God will say that the body of a pig is more suitable for us. We could be born as a pig in the next life. If we make sleeping as our primary goal, then God could put us in the body of a polar bear in the next life, where we could sleep for many months at a stretch.

The Concept of Rebirth

Everyone is born in different circumstances. Someone is born in a rich family and has no shortage of worldly possessions, while another person is born in a poor family where finding food is a daily struggle. Someone is born with a keen intellect and easily excels in studies, while someone is born with a dull mind and cannot do well in studies despite working very hard. How do you explain this inequality? Is it that God is unjust or unfair in handling our affairs? No! This difference is due to the karmas of past lives.

A person, who is blind from birth, may ask, "What did I do for which I am suffering like this?" How would you

answer him? If you say, "It must be the will of God," that would be incorrect. God is all-good, and He does not wish anyone to suffer. If you say, "It is a result of your actions in this life," that would also be incorrect. The person was born blind, and all actions in this life were performed later. The only logical answer is that this is a consequence of the person's actions in past lives. God has kept an account of those actions and given the results.

Religious traditions that do not accept the idea of past lives are unable to answer the above question. A Jewish Rabbi, Harold Kushner, has discussed this issue in his book, "Why Do Bad Things Happen to Good People." He had a son who suffered from a peculiar disease called "Progeria". This disease causes premature ageing. Because of it, Kushner's son started growing old from childhood itself. By the age of fourteen years, he displayed the symptoms of an eighty-year old, and then passed away. Kushner was terribly disturbed by this and could find no suitable answer to why his son suffered in this manner. He thought that if suffering is a consequence of what we do in this life, his son had not done anything so evil as to be given such affliction. However, the Vedic philosophy has a perfectly logical explanation for such a scenario. With the understanding of the concept of multiple births, it explains that suffering can even be a result of sins committed in past lives.

Remembrance of Past Lives

The question can then be asked, that if we have had many lives before this one, then why do we not remember them? This is because of the process of death and birth that we go through at the end and beginning of life. It is said that death is a very painful experience for the soul. It erases most of the memories of that life. Again, the process of birth is an even more painful experience for the soul and it wipes out the remaining recollections of the previous life.

However upon birth, the soul does possess a faint remembrance. If you observe a little baby, you will find that without any apparent reason, it sometimes becomes fearful, sometimes happy, and sometimes it starts crying without a cause. At that time, it is remembering events of past lives and reliving those feelings. As the baby grows older, the impressions of this life are so strong that the fainter impressions of past lives are forgotten.

There are some exceptions to this rule. In all parts of the world, there have occasionally been people who have remembered their past lives. Scientists have examined their statements about their past lives, and confirmed them as true.

Forgetfulness of the Self

Most people are living in a state of forgetfulness of their "self". If you ask car drivers to introduce themselves and they say, "I am a Mercedes," "I am a Ford," "I am a Toyota," etc., you will think it to be gross ignorance. You have asked the drivers for their introduction and they are introducing the cars in which they are seated.

Similarly, if you ask someone to introduce herself, she may respond, "I am Bimala."

"But that is your name. You are not the name. The name was given to you at the age of three. But you existed even before that. I am asking who you are."

"I am an Indian."

"That is your nationality. You could change your nationality to American, but you would still remain the same person. I am asking about YOU."

"I am a schoolgirl."

"That is your status in life. Tomorrow it could change and you could become a college girl. You are not your status in life. Who are you?"

"I am a human."

That is your species. It is the designation of your body. You have no information about yourself?"

In this way, people are confusing the body to be themselves. But this body will be left behind one day. When someone dies, people say, "He left the world." Who has left the world, when the body is lying in the hospital bed? Intuitively they realize that the person was not the body, and hence he is no longer present in the world.

Bodily Happiness Cannot Satisfy the Soul

Now, if we confuse the body to be the self, it leads to compounding problems. This is like a compounding mistake in Mathematics. If you begin your calculations from the equation 2 + 2 = 5, all further multiplications will only compound the error. Similarly, if we think the body to be the self, our goal will be to give happiness to the body.

Most people are in the confusion that bodily happiness is their happiness. They keep planning, "What should I eat to become happy? What should I see to become happy? What should I hear to become happy?" They think that if they get the objects of the bodily senses, this will give them happiness. However, no

matter how much they try, the soul within remains unsatisfied. They spend their entire lives searching for happiness and yet find no satisfaction.

The simple logic is that the body is material and the world is also material. Worldly happiness enjoyed through the body can never satisfy the soul. If you take a fish out of the water, you may massage it in scented oil and put food down its throat, but this will never make it happy. The poor fish cannot speak, but if it could, it would say, "I do not want all this. If you want to make me happy, then put me back into the water."

The soul is Divine, and is a part of God. The happiness it is seeking will also be attained only from God. If we can understand this simple logic, then we will make God-realization the goal of our lives. This is what the Vedic scriptures and all the religions of the world ask us to do. Hence, in the next chapter, we will discuss about God.卐

Chapter 2 The Nature of God

The Creator of the World

Is there a God? If so, who is He? And should we believe in Him merely on faith, or is there any proof of His existence? These questions have been raised innumerable times in history. In the present too, they arise in the minds of many people. Let us begin finding the answers to these questions, from the world around us.

We live in a creation that is so amazing; from the smallest atom to the largest galaxies. How did this world come into existence? Some Scientists propose the "Big Bang" theory to explain creation. They claim that there was a big mass of concentrated matter. It exploded and cooled down as it scattered and, the world came into being. There is a humorous anecdote regarding this theory. James Maxwell, one of the greatest scientists in history, was a firm believer in God. His fellow scientist and close friend did not believe there was a God. He would argue that the world was created by itself. One day, Maxwell made a model of the solar system, and put it in motion in his study room.

His friend came to meet him, and on seeing the model, he exclaimed, "This is amazing! Who made it?"

"Nobody made it," replied Maxwell. "I was working on my table when I heard an explosion. I turned around and saw this had been created."

"How ridiculous," his friend retorted. "How can this be created by an explosion? Definitely, someone must have made it."

James Maxwell said, "My friend, you are not willing to believe that a little model of the solar system could be created by itself. And you want me to believe that the real universe, consisting of many such solar systems has come into existence without a creator. If it is logical to believe that someone has created this model, it is also common-sensical to conclude that the real world must have a Creator too."

This is exactly how the Vedas describe God:

यतो वा इमानि भूतानि जायन्ते येन जातानि जीवन्ति
यत्प्रयन्त्यभिसंविशन्ति। (तैत्तिरीय उपनिषद् ३.१.१)

yato vā imāni bhūtāni jāyante yena jātāni jīvanti
yatprayantyabhisaṁviśhanti (Taittirīya Upanishad 3.1.1)

"God is He, Who has created this world; God is He, within Whom the entire world exists; God is He, within Whom the whole world will merge at the time of annihilation."

One Geography teacher taught her students that the world

was created by itself. She then asked the students to make a map of the world for their homework, and bring it the next day. One of the students disagreed with what the teacher had taught. He decided to play a prank on her.

The next day, he scribbled lines on a sheet of paper and filled it with random colors. He put his sheet in-between the pile of sheets submitted by the other students. The teacher came to the classroom and began correcting the maps before her. When she came to that scrap of paper, she was infuriated. "Who did this!" she exclaimed. The whole class was silent. "Tell me who did it, or I shall punish everyone," she said.

The student who had made it got up. "Ma'am! In my opinion no one made it," he said.

"What do you mean?" asked the teacher.

"I think the paper flew and it fell on your desk," the student replied. "The pencil flew and scribbled lines on it. The colors flew and they got filled in the paper."

How is that possible?" the teacher retorted. "Definitely someone must have made it. And I strongly suspect you must be the one."

"Ma'am! You are not willing to believe that a small map of the planet earth has been made by itself. Yet, you have taught us that the real world consisting of innumerable such planets was created by itself? Just as it is reasonable to assume that the map must have been made by someone, it is also logical to conclude that the actual world must have a Creator."

The *Vedānt Darśhan* gives the definition of God in the same manner. It begins by stating in the first aphorism:

अथातो ब्रह्म जिज्ञासा। (वेदान्त दर्शन १.१.१)

athāto brahma jīgyāsā (Vedānta Darśhana 1.1.1)

"Now try to know God." However, on reading the aphorism, the natural question arises, who is God? This is answered in the second aphorism of the Vedānt Darśhan:

जन्माद्यस्य यतः। (वेदान्त दर्शन १.१.२)

janmādyasya yataḥ (Vedānta Darśhana 1.1.2)

"God is He, Who has created this world."

Many Names of the One God

The Hindus worship Bhagavan, the Christians worship Christ, the Muslims worship Allah, the Jews worship Yahweh, the Parsis worship Ahura Mazda, the Jains worship Alakh Niranjan, the Sikhs worship Ikomkar, and the Buddhists worship Shunya. Are they all different Gods? Often, religious practitioners develop intense enmity against each other on the basis of the God they worship.

The Vedic scriptures give us a broader vision. They clearly state:

एकं सत् विप्रः बहुधा वदन्ति (ऋग् वेद १.१६४.४६)

ekaṁ sat vipraḥ bahudhā vadanti (Ṛig Veda 1.164.46)

"The Absolute Truth is one, but devotees call Him by many names." The Creator of the world is one. All the religions are worshipping the same All-powerful God. Quarrels arise due to lack

of understanding. This is like the story of some blind men, who went to see an elephant. One of them put his hand on the elephant's stomach and exclaimed, "This creature is just like a wall."

The second man caught the leg of the elephant and stated, "This animal is like a tree."

The third caught the tail and said, "The elephant is like a rope."

The fourth caught the elephant's ear and said, "It is like a fan." Now they all started fighting.

This is a Wall
This is a Fan
He is a Tree
It's a Rope

One man with eyes was watching these blind men. He pacified them, "Do not fight. None of you is wrong. You are all describing parts of the same elephant. All that you have said together makes the complete elephant." Similarly, the Vedas, with the eyes of knowledge, tell us not to fight on the basis of religion. They teach us to respect all devotees, explaining that they are all worshipping the same All-powerful Creator, but calling Him by different names.

Can God Have a Form?

Does God have a personal form or not? Some say that He cannot exist in a form. They argue that Krishna, Ram, Shiv, etc. cannot be God, for They possess a form, while God is only formless. Others believe that God does manifest in various forms.

The fact is that God is All-powerful. He has created this world around us, which is full of shapes and forms. If God can create a world filled with forms, does He not have the ability to Himself take on a form? Of course He does. If we claim that He cannot have a form, this implies that we do not accept Him as the All-powerful God. And if we admit that He is All-powerful, then we must also accept that He possesses the power to manifest Himself in a form.

At the same time, God is also formless. He exists everywhere in the world. If He were not formless, then how could His Divine presence be everywhere? If He is all-pervading, then it is necessary that He is formless.

God is perfect and complete, and so He is both—formless and possessing forms. We individual souls too have both aspects to our personality. The soul is formless. Yet, we have taken on human bodies, not once, but innumerable times in countless

lifetimes. If we tiny souls have the ability to take on a form, definitely the All-powerful God can also take on a form, if He wishes. Hence, the Vedas state that there are both aspects to God's personality:

द्वे वाव ब्रह्मणो रूपे मूर्तं चैव अमूर्तं च।
(बृहदारण्यक उपनिषद् २.३.१)

dve vāva brahmaṇo rūpe
mūrtaṁ chaiva amūrtaṁ cha
(Bṛihadāraṇyaka Upanishad 2.3.1)

"God is formless and All-pervading, but He also manifests in a personal form."

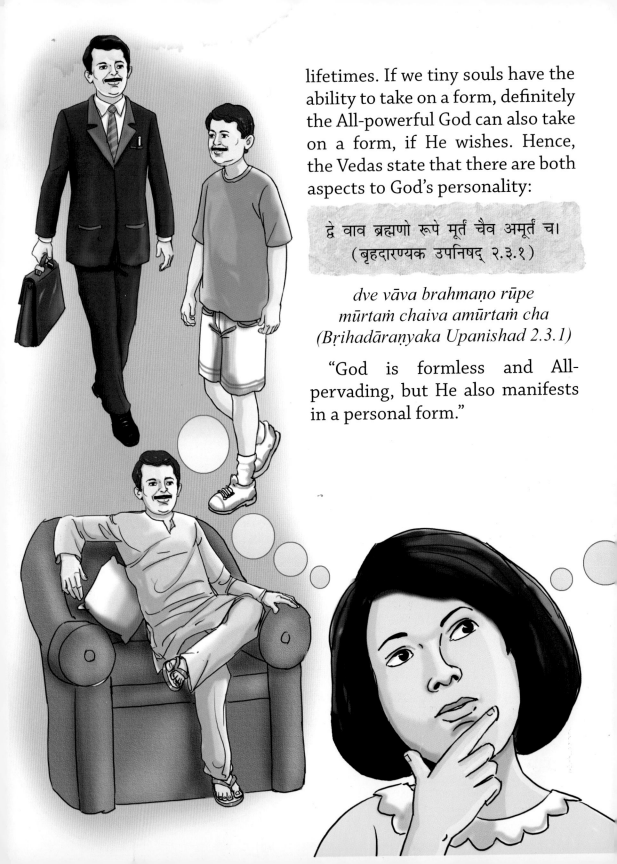

The Many Forms of God

In Hinduism, we have many Gods—Krishna, Ram, Shiv, Vishnu, Durga, etc. Are they all different Gods? And if so, are some of them bigger than the others? The answer is that these are not different Gods. They are different forms of the same Supreme Lord.

We too have many personalities. When your father goes to office, he is dressed very formally. When he takes you out to the park, he is dressed semi-formally. And when he is at home, he is dressed very informally. Now, you do not become confused, thinking how come you have three fathers. You know very well that these are three different appearances of your one father. Similarly, Krishna, Ram, Shiv, Vishnu, etc. are not different Gods; They all are different forms of the same one God.

Hence, we should not consider any one form of God

as bigger and others as smaller. This is stated in the Vedas:

एकं संतम् बहुधाय कल्पयन्ति। (ऋग् वेद १०.११४.५)

ekaṁ santam bahudhāya kalpayanti (Ṛig Veda 10.114.5)

"The Absolute Truth is one but it has been described in a variety of ways by the Saints."

While comparing the example of a worldly father with God, we must also note the difference. A worldly father is not all-powerful; he cannot exist in all three places at the same time. However, God is Supremely powerful. He can manifest in as many forms as He wishes and exist in all of them simultaneously. Therefore, He eternally exists in the forms of Krishna, Ram, Shiv, Vishnu, etc. The true devotee respects all these forms of God, although doing devotion to any one of Them.

The Celestial gods

What about the celestial *devatās* such as *Indra, Varuṇ, Kuber, Agni, Vāyu*, etc.? What is their status in comparison to the Supreme God? These *devatās* live in the higher planes of existence

within this material world, called swarg, or the celestial abodes. The *devatās* are not God; they are souls like all of us. They occupy specific posts in the affairs of running the world.

Consider the Federal government of the country. There is a Secretary of State, a Finance Secretary, an Industries Secretary, an Agriculture Secretary, and so on. These are posts, and chosen people occupy those posts for a limited tenure. At the end of the tenure, the government changes and all the post-holders change too. The posts of Secretary of State etc. remain but the persons holding those posts change.

Similarly, in the governance of the affairs of the world, there are posts such as *Agni Dev* (the god of fire), *Vāyu Dev* (the god of the wind), *Varuṇ Dev* (the god of the ocean), *Indra Dev* (the king of the celestial gods), etc. Souls selected by virtue of their deeds in past lives occupy these seats for a certain amount of time. Then they fall from their posts and others occupy these seats. Thus, souls get these posts of *Agni Dev, Vāyu Dev, Indra Dev, Varuṇ Dev,* etc. only temporarily. We cannot compare them to the Supreme Lord. This distinction should be borne in mind between the various forms of *Bhagavān*, or God, and the celestial gods, or *devatās* of swarg.

Many people worship the celestial gods for material rewards. However, we must remember that these *devatās* cannot grant either liberation from material bondage or God-realization. Even if they do bestow material benefits, it is only by the powers they have received from God. Hence, Shree Krishna says in the Bhagavad Geeta that people who worship the celestial gods are less intelligent. Those who are situated in knowledge, worship the Supreme Lord.卐

Chapter 3 The Goal of Life

The Importance of Setting Our Goal

Human life is a rare opportunity presented by God to the soul. The other species, such as plants, fishes, birds, reptiles, insects, and mammals, have only sufficient knowledge to survive. They cannot ask philosophic questions related to God, the soul, Divine love, and the goal of life. They do not have sufficient knowledge to ponder over these topics.

Even if they could, they would not be able to do anything about it. They do not possess the ability to go against their basic instincts. For example, a lion is carnivorous by nature. It

cannot willfully decide to go on a vegetarian diet for spiritual progress. On the other hand, humans possess both—the power of knowledge and the ability to control their mind and intellect. Hence, human beings can willfully decide their goal in life and strive to attain it.

Many humans have never thought about their goal, and they wander purposelessly through life. This is like the traveler who asked a bystander whether he was on the right path. The bystander asked him where he wished to go. The traveler replied

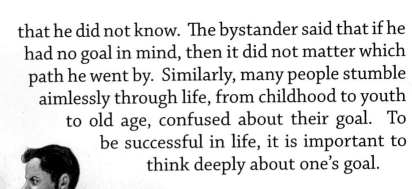

that he did not know. The bystander said that if he had no goal in mind, then it did not matter which path he went by. Similarly, many people stumble aimlessly through life, from childhood to youth to old age, confused about their goal. To be successful in life, it is important to think deeply about one's goal.

The Search for Happiness

What is it that we are all looking for? The Vedic scriptures say that we are all seeking happiness in everything we do. We may have different decisions regarding where happiness lies. Someone feels that if only he could get a bigger car, he would be happy. Another person thinks that if she could get a nice house, she would be happy. Someone else believes that by becoming rich, he would be happy, while yet another feels that if only she could become a movie star, she would be happy. However, everyone's goal is happiness, and twenty-four hours a day, all that we do is for its sake.

We all know that we want happiness, but to deepen our understanding about happiness, let us ponder over a question. Did anybody teach us to seek happiness, just as we had to learn everything else? We were taught, "My child! You should always speak the truth." "Son, you should never speak lies." "My daughter, you should never steal from anyone." We had to learn how to read, write, and speak. In the same way, did we have to be taught, "My child! You must always seek happiness. It should not come about that you start loving misery." This instruction was never given to us. Without ever being taught to do so, we naturally began seeking bliss.

In fact, the moment we were born, the first thing we did was to express our desire for happiness. We did not say it in words, since we could not speak. We did it by crying out with all our might. That is the first thing a child does when it comes into this world. Why does the child cry on birth? In the process of birth, it experiences pain, and it cries to reveal its nature. "I have not come into this world for pain. I have come for bliss. Give me happiness!" Since then, until this day, all we have done is for the sake of happiness. Hence, we can safely conclude that the goal of all living beings is happiness.

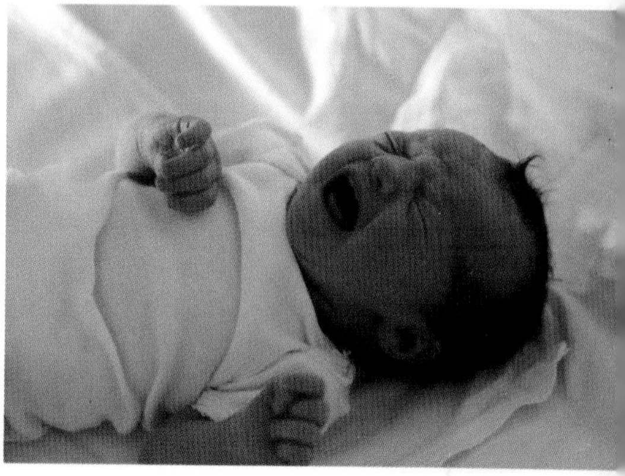

God is an Ocean of Divine Bliss

Why do we all want happiness? In the entire world, the answer to this question is only found in the Vedic scriptures. They declare that we are all looking for happiness because God is an ocean of happiness.

आनन्दो ब्रह्मेति व्यजानात्। (तैत्तिरीय उपनिषद् ३.६)

ānando brahmeti vyajānāt (Taittirīya Upanishad 3.6)

आनन्दमयोऽभ्यासात्। (वेदान्त दर्शन १.१.१२)

ānandamayo 'bhyāasāt (Vedānta Darśhana 1.1.12)

आनन्द सिंधु मध्य तव वासा।। (रामायण)

ānanda siñdhu madhya tava vāsā (Ramayan)

Ānand means Bliss, and the above verses from the Vedic scriptures state that God is an ocean of unlimited Bliss.

We souls are tiny parts of God, and hence we are all tiny parts of the ocean of Bliss. Shree Krishna told Arjun:

ममैवांशो जीवलोके जीवभूतः सनातनः। (भगवद् गीता १५.७)

mamaivānśho jīvaloke jīvabhūtaḥ sanātanaḥ (Geeta 15.7)

"All the souls in the world are My eternal parts." For example, a piece of stone is a part of the mountain, a drop of water is a part of the ocean, and a ray of light is a part of the sun. Similarly, we souls are small fragments of God.

Now, every part is naturally attracted towards its source. A lump of mud is a part of the earth and it is drawn towards it. If you throw it up, it will automatically fall down, pulled by the gravitational force of the earth. Newton discovered this gravitational force when an apple fell on his head.

Similarly, rivers are parts of the ocean and are pulled towards it. They were created from the water vapor that rose from the ocean, and then formed into clouds and rained on the earth. Hence, rivers naturally flow towards the ocean, which is their source. In the same way, the soul is naturally attracted towards its source, which is God. And since, God is the ocean of Bliss, the soul is drawn towards Bliss. This is the explanation to the question why we all have the desire for happiness within us.

The Way to Attain Perfect Happiness

Although we have been searching for happiness, we have still not attained it. No matter how many worldly pleasures we may enjoy, the feeling of dissatisfaction remains. The reason is that worldly pleasures give only a fleeting experience of enjoyment. For example someone says, "I had a great time yesterday. We went to the football game and had a lot of fun."

You ask him, "What happened today?"

He says, "Today my car was out-of-order. So I stayed at home. The TV was also not working, and I got terribly bored."

"So the happiness of yesterday went away today?"

"Yes it did."

"That kind of happiness, which comes and goes, cannot satisfy you."

Our soul is looking for happiness that will remain forever, and which is unlimited in extent. Such happiness is the Bliss of God. Our desire for bliss will only be fulfilled when we attain God. This desire for bliss is, knowingly or unknowingly, a desire for the ocean of Bliss—God Himself. The ancient poet Valmiki says:

लोके नहि स विद्येत यो न राममनुव्रतः।। (रामायण)

loke nahi sa vidyeta yo na rāmamanuvrataḥ (Ramayan)

There is no soul in this world who is not a devotee of Lord Ram. Even if one tries for many ages, one cannot desire anything apart from God, because one cannot desire the reverse of happiness, which is misery.

Our Love for Godly Qualities

Besides happiness, we also naturally love godly virtues, such as truthfulness, non-violence, justice, kindness, etc. You may ask, "How is that so? Not everyone is truthful. There are so many people in this world who are habitual liars".

Definitely, there are liars in this world. However, if you lie to them, will they like it? No, they will object, "Why did you lie to me?"

"But you speak lies yourself?"

"Yes I do, but I want everyone to be truthful to me."

In English language, there is an expression, "Honesty amongst thieves." If a member of a gang of thieves speaks a lie to the gang leader, he gets annoyed. Even the leader amongst thieves wants truthful behavior from others.

A thief once stole from someone's house and returned to his home. He counted his loot and went to sleep, satisfied that he had committed a successful robbery. At night, another thief entered his house and stole from him. When the first thief woke up and realized that his house had been burgled, he exclaimed, "Who did this? Does he not know who I am? If I find him, I will kill him."

Ask him, "You are a thief yourself, why are you getting so annoyed?" "That is okay. I may steal from others, but I do not want anyone to steal from me."

The examples illustrate that everyone desires kind, just, and honest behavior from others, no matter how unjust, unkind, or dishonest they may themselves be. Why is this so? The reason is that these godly virtues are the qualities of God. We are all His tiny parts, so we inherently love godly qualities. This explains why we want virtuous behavior from others. It again goes to show that, knowingly or unknowingly, we are all searching for God.

We can thus conclude that the goal of our life is to realize God. Only on attaining Him, can we experience the peace, contentment, happiness, and satisfaction that our soul has been searching for since endless lifetimes. Once we have decided that God-realization is the aim of our life, we then have to learn, from the Vedic scriptures, how to attain it. We will discuss this in the next chapter. 卐

Chapter 4

Vedas– The Eternal Knowledge of God

The Importance of the Vedas

We would like to know where God stays. What does He do? What does He look like? And so on. To learn any subject, such as Physics, Chemistry, and Mathematics, etc., we read textbooks. From where can we learn the subject of God? Are there any books we can refer to? These books should have been written by someone who knows God and whom we can trust. They should have no scope for mistakes.

Such books are the Vedas. These Vedas are not the works of any human being; God has Himself produced them. If they had been created by any human, one could have had doubts about what was written in them. However, when the author is God Himself, then all doubts cease. Besides, who can know God better than Himself? Hence, what the Vedas say about God is the perfect reference source for spiritual knowledge. Since they have been manifest by God, they are considered the most sacred amongst the Hindu scriptures and are given the highest place. These Vedas are the ultimate authority in Hinduism.

भूतं भव्यं भविष्यं च सर्वं वेदात् प्रसिध्यति।। (मनु स्मृति १२.९७)

bhūtaṁ bhavyaṁ bhaviṣhyaṁ cha sarvaṁ vedāt prasidhyati
(Manu Smṛiti 12.97)

"Any spiritual principle is only acceptable if it is in conformity with the Vedas."

History of the Vedas

Strictly speaking, the Vedas are not the name of any books. They are the Divine knowledge of God. They have existed ever since God has existed, i.e. since eternity. Each time God creates the world, He reveals the Vedas in the heart of Brahma, the first created being. The Vedic knowledge is then passed down from Brahma, via Guru to disciple, through word of mouth. Hence, another name for the Vedas is *Śhruti*, or knowledge conveyed by hearing.

About 5000 years ago, the sage Ved Vyas, who was an Avatar of God, put the same Vedic knowledge down in writing. He also divided the Vedas, which was one body of knowledge, into four parts—*Ṛig Veda, Yajur Veda, Sāma Veda*, and *Atharva Veda*. Hence, He came to be known as Ved Vyas, or "The one, who divided the Vedas into four parts."

Modern day scholars recognize the Ṛig Veda as the oldest

book and most ancient poetry of humankind. However, the words "oldest" and "ancient" are not accurate descriptions of its antiquity. The Vedas are *Sanātan*, or eternal, just as God Himself is eternal. Therefore, the path to God-realization, that the Vedas describe, is called *Sanātan Dharm*, or "Eternal religion." Other religious traditions have had a beginning in history, while *Sanātan Dharm* has always existed.

Language of the Vedas

The Vedas have been written in Sanskrit, which is the language of the celestial abodes. Even modern linguists acknowledge that Sanskrit has the most systematic grammar in the world. Computer scientists declare Sanskrit to be the most computer-friendly language. Its grammar is so sophisticated that the course for learning it is of twelve-year duration. Historians are amazed how people 5000 years ago, could speak a language with such complex grammatical rules!

Sanskrit is also recognized as the mother of all languages. All the Indian languages, such as Tamil, Telugu, Kannada, Marathi, Oriya, Bengali, Gujarati, Punjabi, Marwari, etc., have originated from Sanskrit. All languages of the western world, such as English, German, French, Spanish, etc., have originated from Latin. Now the interesting thing is that if we compare Latin with Sanskrit, it becomes obvious that Latin has originated from Sanskrit. Many words of Sanskrit found their way in Latin. Also, the Latin grammar is a watered-down version of the Sanskrit grammar. This fact has been acknowledged by many Western scholars, as stated below:

"India was the motherland of our race, and Sanskrit the mother of Europe's languages: She was the mother of our philosophy; mother, through the Arabs, of much of our Mathematics; mother, through the Buddha, of the ideals embodied in Christianity; mother, through the village community, of self-governance and democracy. Mother India is in many ways the mother of us all." Will Durant, American Historian and Philosopher, World-famous author of "The Story of Philosophy" (1885-1981).

Sir William Jones

"The Sanskrit language, whatever be its antiquity, is of wonderful structure; more perfect than Greek, more copious than Latin, and more exquisitely refined than either." Sir William Jones, English philologist, master of thirteen languages and knower of twenty-eight more (1746 to 1794).

Sections of the Vedas

Each Veda contains four sections: *Sanhitā, Brāhmaṇa, Āraṇyak,* and Upanishad.

1. ***Sanhitā***: These contain hymns or mantras addressed to various celestial gods, and to the Supreme Lord.

2. ***Brāhmaṇa***: These describe the rituals, such as the yagyas, or fire sacrifices, in which these hymns are employed.

3. ***Āraṇyak***: These discuss the meanings of the rituals and lead to philosophic enquiry.

4. **Upanishad**: These are the philosophical texts revealing knowledge of God.

Vedāṅga

These are supplementary to the Vedas; they assist in understanding the Vedas. There are six *Vedāṅgas*:

1. ***Śhikṣhā***: It contains the rules of chanting the mantras.

2. ***Kalp***: It contains the rules for performing the rituals.

3. ***Vyākaraṇa***: It contains the grammar of the Vedas.

4. ***Nirukti***: It is the dictionary of the Vedas.

5. ***Chhand***: It is the study of the scales, melodies, and meters in which the Vedic mantras are sung.

6. ***Jyotiṣh***: These are astrological texts.

Other Vedic Scriptures

Although the Vedas are the ultimate source of spiritual knowledge, they are not easy to understand. To elaborate their meaning, many more scriptures have been written. These scriptures do not deviate from the authority of the Vedas. Rather, they attempt to elaborate and explain the meaning of the Vedas. The most important amongst these are the *Itihās* and the *Purāṇas*. The Upanishads accord the *Itihās* and the *Purāṇas*, the status of the fifth Veda:

इतिहासपुराणं पञ्चमं वेदानां वेदं (छान्दोग्य उपनिषद् ७.१.२)

itihāsapurāṇaṁ pañchamaṁ vedānāṁ vedaṁ
(Chhāndogya Upanishad 7.1.2)

"Know the *Itihās* and *Purāṇas* to be the fifth Veda." Reading them helps clarify the meaning of the Vedas.

This is just as there is the constitution of the land, describing in its various statuettes, the complex laws of the land. Then there are also commentaries written on the constitution by senior advocates. The constitution is often difficult to understand, and so to comprehend it, commentaries are consulted. The commentaries clarify the meaning even better than the constitution itself and many students read only the commentaries, without feeling any need to read the constitution. Similarly, the *Purāṇas* and *Itihās* reveal the purport of the Vedas.

Itihās

These are the historical texts, and are two in number—the Ramayan and the Mahabharat. They describe the history related to two important Descensions of God.

The Ramayan has been written by the Sage Valmiki, and describes the *leelas*, or Divine pastimes of Lord Ram. Amazingly, it was written by Valmiki before Shree Ram actually displayed His

leelas. The great poet Sage was empowered with Divine vision, by which he could see the pastimes Lord Ram would enact on descending in the world. He thus put them down in 24,000 most beautifully composed Sanskrit verses of the Ramayan. These verses also contain lessons on ideal behavior in various social roles, such as son, brother, wife, king, and married couples.

The Ramayan has also been written in many regional languages of India, thereby increasing its popularity amongst the people. The most famous amongst these is the Hindi Ramayan, Ramcharit Manas, written by a great devotee of Lord Ram, Saint Tulsidas.

The Mahabharat has been written by the sage Ved Vyas. It contains 100,000 verses and is considered the longest poem in

the world. The Divine *leelas*, or pastimes, of Lord Krishna are the central theme of the Mahabharat. It is full of wisdom and guidance related to duties in all stages of human life, and devotion to God.

The Bhagavad Geeta is a portion of the Mahabharat. It contains a dialogue between Lord Krishna and Arjun, before the beginning of the war of Mahabharat. The Bhagavad Geeta is the most popular Hindu scripture, since it contains the essence of spiritual knowledge, so nicely described by Lord Krishna Himself. It has been translated in almost every language of the world. Innumerable commentaries have been written on the Bhagavad Geeta.

Purāṇas

There are eighteen *Purāṇas*, written by the sage Ved Vyas. Together, they contain 400,000 verses. These describe the Divine pastimes of the various forms of God and His devotees. The *Purāṇas* are also full of philosophic knowledge. They discuss the creation of the universe, its annihilation and recreation, the history of humankind, the genealogy of the celestial gods and the holy sages, etc.

The most important amongst them is the *Bhāgavat Purāṇa*, or the Shreemad Bhagavatam. It was the last scripture written by sage Ved Vyas. In it, he mentions that in this scripture, he is going to reveal the highest dharm of pure selfless love for God. Philosophically, where the Bhagavad Geeta ends, the Shreemad Bhagavatam begins.

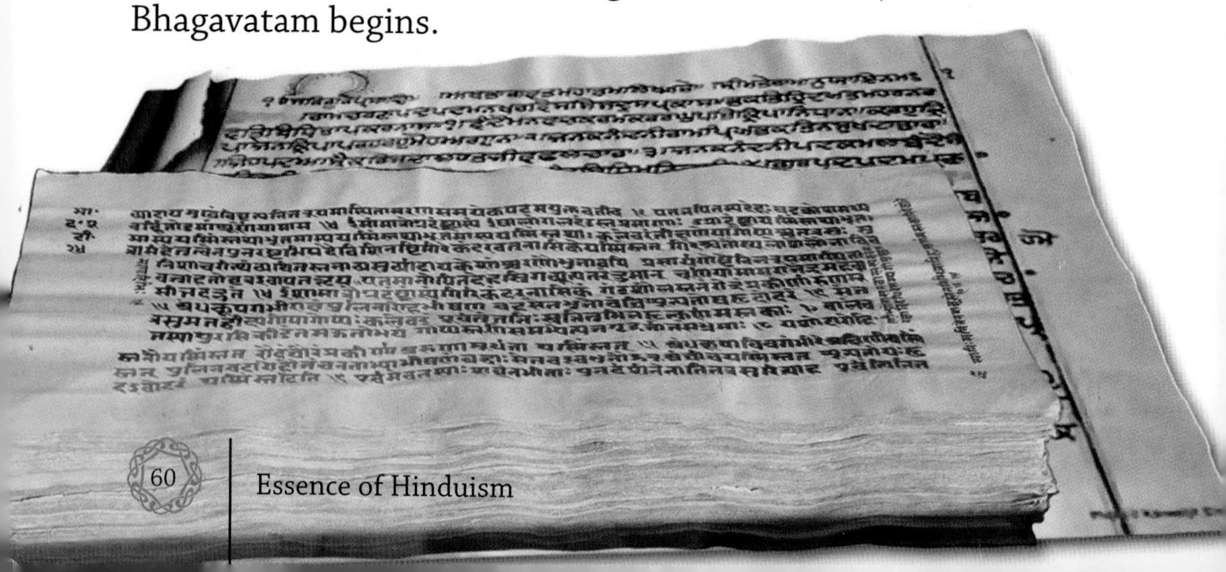

The *Purāṇas* and the *Itihās* are parts of the *Smṛiti* texts. *Smṛitis* are those scriptures that have not been directly manifested by God. They contain knowledge that was revealed in the heart of sages, who then put it down in writing. Since the sages remembered this knowledge on the inspiration of God, these scriptures are called *Smṛiti*.

Ṣhaḍ-darśhan

These come next in importance amongst the Vedic scriptures. Six sages wrote six scriptures, highlighting particular aspects of Hindu philosophy. These became known as the *ṣhaḍ-darśhan*, or six philosophic works. They are:

1. ***Mimānsā Darśhan*:** It was written by *Maharṣhi* (Sage) Jaimini. It describes ritualistic duties and ceremonies.

2. ***Vedānt Darśhan*:** It was written by *Maharṣhi* Ved Vyas. It discusses the nature of the Absolute Truth.

3. ***Nyāya Darśhan*:** It was written by *Maharṣhi* Gautam. It develops a system of logic for understanding life and the Absolute Truth.

4. ***Vaiśheṣhik Darśhan*:** It was written by *Maharṣhi* Kanad. It analyses cosmology and creation from the perspective of its various elements.

5. ***Yog Darśhan*:** It was written by *Maharṣhi* Patanjali. It describes an eightfold path to union with God, beginning with physical postures.

6. ***Sānkhya Darśhan*:** It was written by *Maharṣhi* Kapil. It describes the evolution of the Universe from *prakṛiti*, the primordial form of the material energy.

Apart from the scriptures mentioned above, there are

hundreds of others in the Hindu tradition. It would be impossible to describe them all here. Let it suffice to say that the Vedic scriptures are a vast treasure-house of Divine knowledge revealed by God and the Saints for the eternal welfare of all humankind.

Scriptures of Other Religions

Hindus respect the scriptures of all religions. Yet, we must bear in mind the specialty of the Vedic scriptures. Any teacher is constrained to reveal knowledge according to the level of the students. The teacher may be Ph.D. but if she is teaching first grade students, she will only teach 2 + 2 = 4. This does not mean that the teacher only knows that much, rather the students can only understand up to that level. Likewise, there is a gradation in the scriptures of the world, based on the circumstance and the need of the times.

The Koran was revealed for people living in the desert, who were leading a very crude lifestyle. Hence, Islam teaches a very rudimentary philosophy. Followers are repeatedly scolded to worship Allah out of fear of going to Hell. Again, the temptation offered is that if they have faith, they will go to Heaven, where

GENESIS
"He will keep you strong to the end, so that you will be blameless on the day of our Lord Jesus Christ."
1 Corinthians 1:8 (niv)

they will enjoy worldly delights. The concept of selfless love for God is left untouched.

The Bible too gives this impetus of Heaven and Hell, but to a lesser extent. It starts emphasizing pure devotion to God a little more. It also mentions basic morality, such as: "Thou shall not steal thy neighbor's manservant, maidservant, ox, or ass (Ten Commandments)." However, the Bible too was spoken to fishermen in the desert. Hence, the highest truths of God-realization could not be revealed in it.

Now, the listener of the Bhagavad Geeta is Arjun, who is a highly evolved soul. If Shree Krishna had instructed him, "Thou shall not steal," Arjun would have felt offended. "Why is He instructing me like that? Does He doubt that I will steal?" To such an advanced student as Arjun, Shree Krishna spoke the Bhagavad Geeta, which deals with the fine science of God-realization. Hence, it is said that where the Koran Sharif ends, the Bible begins; and where the Bible ends, the Bhagavad Geeta begins.

Even beyond the Bhagavad Geeta is the Shreemad Bhagavatam. It was spoken by Sage Shukadev to Parikshit, who was totally detached from the world. He had only seven days to live, and had renounced his kingdom to hear the Bhagavatam. Hence, where the Bhagavad Geeta ends, the Shreemad Bhagavatam begins.

The spectrum of Vedic scriptures is like a general merchant's shop. They contain instructions for all the classes, starting from the most basic, all the way up to the most advanced. We have to see what class we are in, and follow the instructions appropriate to our class. Hence, it is recommended that we learn Vedic scriptures under the guidance of a Guru, or spiritual teacher.

The Need for a Guru

Although we do consult books to acquire knowledge about a subject, they usually do not suffice. We also need a teacher who can explain the complex content of the books. Besides, while reading them, innumerable doubts arise in the mind. The teacher helps us resolve these doubts and attain clarity in our understanding.

Similarly, the Vedic scriptures are a treasure-house of Divine knowledge. However, there are so many scriptures and the knowledge in them is so sublime that it is not easy to comprehend them on our own. Their complexities can easily baffle down an unguided reader. Hence, all the Vedic scriptures themselves instruct that we should understand them under the guidance of a Spiritual Master, or Guru.

आचार्यवान् पुरुषो वेदः। (छान्दोग्य उपनिषद् ६.१४.२)

āchāryavān puruṣho vedaḥ (Chhāndogya Upanishad 6.14.2)

The Vedas say, "One who studies the Vedas under the guidance of an *Āchārya,* can understand their meaning." This topic of Guru will be discussed later in the book. Let us now find out, from these Vedic scriptures, about the way to reach God.卐

Chapter 5 Grace of God

Knowledge Leads to Love

The Vedas inform us that if we wish to attain God, we must first acquire knowledge of Him. When we know Him, we will develop faith in Him, and through faith, we will develop love for Him. Understand this principle through a worldly example.

Let us say that you were celebrating your birthday party. Your friends were coming one-by-one, greeting you and offering you their birthday gifts. Someone came and gave a dirty cloth bundle. You looked at it and curled your nose in distaste, thinking, "What is this dirty bundle?"

The person said, "Don't jump to conclusions. Take a look inside."

You removed the cloth and found a million dollars inside. On finding out, you immediately wrapped it up again and placed it against your heart. "Wow! This is a real gift. With this, I can buy anything I want."

When you had no knowledge of the gift you had received, you had no love for it. When you came to know its worth, you immediately developed love for it. How did this come about? Knowledge created faith, and faith created love. Similarly, if we can come to know of the greatness of God, the powers that He possesses, the incredible things that He does, and how glorious He is, we will naturally develop faith in Him. Then, through faith, we will develop love.

Knowledge Makes Us Grateful

Consider another example. Someone had a car accident in the countryside. His car hit a lamppost and got crushed. The man fainted unconscious inside the car. A villager came to the rescue. He checked the man's pockets, and finding his home address, informed his relatives about the accident. The villager then lifted him up, put him in his own car, and drove him to the nearest hospital. On checking the patient, the doctor said that to save his life, blood was required immediately. The villager donated his own blood, which turned out to be of a matching blood group.

When the man came back to consciousness, he found his relatives in the hospital room. He was overjoyed

to see them. However, on noticing the villager, he frowned in distaste, "What is this rustic doing in my room?"

The man's relatives informed him, "This is the man who saved your life. He brought you to the hospital, donated his blood for you, and informed us about your accident. If it had not been for him, you would not have lived today."

The man felt deeply indebted, "I am thankful to you with all my heart. There is no way I can repay my debt to you." Without knowledge of what the villager had done for him, the man had curled his lips towards him. Simply by coming to know, he developed such gratitude towards him.

In the same way, if we do not know who God is, how He is related to us, and what He does for us, we too will have no faith or love for Him. But with knowledge of this, we will naturally develop great love for Him. Hence, the Ramayan states:

जानें बिनु न होइ परतीती। बिनु परतीति होइ नहिं प्रीती।। (रामायण)

jāneñ binu na hoi paratītī, binu paratīti hoi nahiñ prītī (Ramayan)

"Knowledge will lead to faith, and faith will lead to love." The next question then is how can we know God?

God is Beyond Our Senses, Mind, and Intellect

We possess three instruments of knowledge—senses, mind, and intellect. If I were to show you a watch, and ask you what it was, you would immediately reply, "It is a wristwatch." How did you find this out? You saw the object with your eyes. The eyes sent information of the image to the mind. The mind then processed that information, to understand its shape, size, color, etc. The processed information was sent to the intellect, which analyzed the data and made a decision that the object was a wristwatch. This is how the organs of knowledge, the senses mind, and intellect work.

These senses, mind, and intellect are incapable of knowing God, because they are all made from the material energy, called Maya. But God is not material, He is Divine, and so He is beyond the senses, mind, and intellect. If you were asked to close your eyes, and read with your ear, you would reply, "This is not possible. The ears cannot see; they perceive sound. The eyes perceive images." In the same way, the material senses, mind, and intellect can only perceive material things. They cannot perceive the Divine God, who is beyond the realm of Maya.

Does that mean we will never attain God? Definitely not! Innumerable Saints in India, such as Shankaracharya, Madhvacharya, Nimbarkacharya, Chaitanya Mahaprabhu, Vallabhacharya, Soordas, Tulsidas, Meerabai, Tukaram, Kabirdas, Guru Nanak, etc. have seen God, spoken to Him, known Him, and realized Him. On what basis did they do so? To find the answer to this riddle, we must once again turn to the Vedas. They are the ultimate authority on the knowledge of God.

Know God through His Grace

The *Atharva Veda* states:

नायमात्मा प्रवचनेन लभ्यो न मेधया न बहुना श्रुतेन।
यमेवैष वृणुते तेन लभ्यस्तस्यैष आत्मा विवृणुते तनूँ स्वाम्।।
(कठ उपनिषद् १.२.२३)

nāyamātmā pravachanena labhyo na medhayā na bahunā śhrutena
yamevaiṣha vṛiṇute tena labhyastasyaiṣha ātmā vivṛiṇute tanūṁ svām
(Kaṭha Upanishad 1.2.23)

"You cannot know God by your self-effort or any other means. Only by His Grace can He be known."

The *Yajur Veda* states the same thing:

तस्य नो रास्व तस्य नो धेहि।

tasya no rāsva tasya no dhehi

"Without the Grace of the lotus feet of God, nobody can know Him." The same verdict is given by the Shreemad Bhagavatam, Bhagavad Geeta, Ramayan, and the others scriptures as well.

When God bestows His Grace, He will add His Divine power to our material senses, mind, and intellect. Equipped with His power, we will be able to see Him, hear Him, know Him, and attain Him. Those fortunate souls, who received His Grace, became God-realized Saints. We did not receive it, and so we remained in material consciousness.

On understanding the principle of Grace, a natural question arises: If God-realization depends upon Grace, then is there no need for self-effort? Can we simply sit down and wait for the Grace, or do we need to do something to receive that Grace? This question will be addressed next.卐

Chapter 6

The Importance of Self-Effort

The Importance of Self-Effort

So far, we have understood that we need Grace to attain the goal of life. Does this mean that there is no importance of our own effort? Should we then stop all our efforts and simply wait for God's Grace? Understand the answer to this question through a humorous story.

A villager had loaded his bullock cart with wheat bags and was bringing it to town. On the way, the wheels of the bullock cart got stuck in the mud. The villager was spiritually inclined and was a devotee of Hanuman. He took out the Hanumān Chālīsā, a prayer book to Hanuman, and began reading it. After completing it, he folded his hands and prayed, "O Hanuman ji! Please come and take my cart out from the mud."

Then he started reciting the Hanumān Chālīsā once more. On completing, he again said, "O Hanuman ji! Please get me out of

this fix and remove my cart from the mud."

Hanuman ji was hearing the pleas of the villager. He thought, "This person is devoted, but his understanding of God's Grace is incorrect. Let me teach him." Hanuman ji manifested before the villager and said, "My dear fellow, if I start taking out people's carts in this manner, the whole world will become lazy. You do this much from your side. Stand with your feet in the mud and push the cart with all your might, while calling out to the bulls. Simultaneously, pray to Me for My Grace. Then I will respond by adding My strength to yours and you will be able to take the cart out. But if you think you will not do anything and Hanuman ji alone should do it, that will never be."

The story illustrates that the Grace of God is necessary but our effort is also required. The Vedas say:

तपःप्रभवाद्देवप्रसादाच्च (श्वेताश्वतर उपनिषद् ६.२१)

tapaḥprabhavāddevaprasādāchcha
(Śhvetāśhvatara Upanishad 6.21)

"Our own effort and the Grace of God are both essential for attaining the Ultimate Goal."

We Have the Free Will to Act

Many people diminish the need for self-effort in their minds by saying, "Nothing is in our hands after all. God is seated within us. He is the doer of all our actions, and we act as He inspires us." However, this philosophy is incorrect, as the following points will illustrate:

1. If God were the doer of all our actions, we would never have committed any mistakes. All of our actions would have

been perfect, since God can never make a blunder. The fact that we make innumerable mistakes implies that we are performing actions with our own free will.

2. If God were the doer of our actions, we would not have to bear the karmic reactions. Why would we suffer for actions that God did through us? He would either bear the karmic reactions on His own, or forgive Himself. But there is the Law of Karma, "As you do, so you shall reap." This implies that we ourselves are the doers of our actions.

3. God is impartial towards all souls and perfectly just. If He was the doer of our actions, He would either have made everyone do good work and become Saints, or He would have made everyone do bad actions and become demons. But there is so much of variety in the world. One is a Saint, like Prahlad, while the other is a demon, like Hiranyakashipu. This variety implies that we have the freedom to choose our own actions, and we are responsible for them, not God.

4. If God were the inspirer of our actions, there would have be no need for Him to reveal the Vedas or any other scriptures. There would be no need for Him to explain to us the path to perfection. He would simply have to say two sentences: "O souls, I am the doer of everything. So there is no need for you to understand what proper and improper action is."

It is true that God is seated within us, and He gives us the power to act. However, what we do with that power is decided by our own free will. This is just as the powerhouse supplies electricity to your house. If it did not give the power, you would not have been able to do any electric work. However, once you have power supply at your home, what you do with it, is your own choice. You could operate the fan, light the lamp, or heat

or cool the house, as you wish. Similarly, God gives our eyes the power to see, but what we see is our own choice. We could go to the temple and see the Deities, or we could go on the internet and see dirty pictures. God is merely giving us the faculty of sight. He is not deciding how you choose to use it.

Hence, we must not blame God for our mistakes. If we do something wrong, we should take responsibility for the error. Only then will we strive to correct it.

Destiny versus Self-effort

Some people do not blame God for their mistakes; they hold their destiny responsible for it. They say that we were all born with our own individual destiny, and our wealth in life, education, fame, life span, and health, are all determined by destiny. Whatever is written in our destiny will happen, no matter what we do; and what is not written, we will never get it, no matter how hard we try. Hence, there is no point in putting

FOLK TALES

effort to accomplish anything.

However, this is an incorrect understanding. Thinking in such a manner will make us lazy. We will assume that everything is decided by destiny, and it does not matter whether we work hard or not. Such debilitating thoughts will impede our efforts and inspiration to work hard. To prevent this, let us try and understand what destiny truly is.

There are three kinds of karmas associated with all of us:

Sañchit karma: All the actions that we have performed in endless lives are noted by God, Who maintains their account. These are called *sañchit* karmas.

Prārabdh karma: At the time of birth, God takes a portion from these accumulated karmas and gives the karmic reactions to us. This becomes our destiny in the present life, and is called *prārabdh* (fate).

Kriyamāṇ karma: *Prārabdh* is decided at birth and is fixed, but we still retain the freedom to perform new karmas. The actions that we do in the present out of our own free will are called *kriyamāṇ* karma. These are not pre-determined; they are in our own hands.

What we get in life is a result of both—the *prārabdh* and the *kriyamāṇ*. Compare this with playing a game of cards. The hand of cards that is dealt to you, is fixed. However, how you play is up to you. If you are a good player, you could win with bad cards, while if you are a bad player, you could lose even with good cards. Similarly, if you put in proper effort, you could succeed despite a bad *prārabdh* (destiny), but if you are lazy, you may fail despite a good *prārabdh*.

So destiny does exist, but with sufficient efforts, we can change

it. We do not need to worry what is written in our destiny, for that will be given to us automatically. The present effort is in our hands and we must do our best in the present moment, to make a bright future.

The Grace of God Must be Deserved

In conclusion, the concept of Grace of God should not diminish the need for self-effort in our minds. God is causelessly merciful, and is waiting to bestow His Grace upon us, but He can only do so when we have a proper vessel for it. If you went to a milkman with a leaking vessel and asked for a liter of milk, the milkman would say, "I am ready to give it to you but you will not be able to retain it. Bring a proper vessel and I will pour it in."

Similarly, we too have to prepare the vessel of our heart to receive the Grace of God. How then do we become qualified for His Grace? This is the next question that we must address.卐

Chapter 7 Surrender to God

God is Perfectly Fair

We have so far understood that God can only be known by His Grace. We must now try to find out how to receive His Grace. If God is causelessly merciful, why has He not bestowed His mercy upon us until now? In addition, if He is impartial, why has He bestowed His Grace on innumerable Saints? What did they do to receive His Grace? And what did we not do that we are bereft of it?

The answer to these questions is that God is just and unbiased. He has His laws based on which He administers the world. If He were to start whimsically bestowing His Grace, people would lose their faith in Him. Consider the following example. A father had two sons. He instructed both of them to go and work hard in his cornfields. The first son obeyed his father's instructions and toiled all day long in the fields. When he returned home, his father said, "Well done my son! Here are two hundred dollars. Go and enjoy yourself."

The second son did not go to the fields. He stayed back home and lay on his bed, watching the television. He also drank liquor and abused his father in a drunken state. At the end of the day, the father rewarded the second son in the same manner. He said, "Never mind! After all, you are also my son. Here, take two hundred dollars and have a good time." The consequence was that the first son lost his motivation to serve and obey his father. He thought, "If that is the reward policy of my father, then there is no point in working hard. My father will give the two hundred dollars in any case."

Similarly, God says that He has kept a condition for bestowing His Grace. If He were to bestow it even on those who did not fulfill the condition, then the God-realized Saints would have complained, "My Lord, we endeavored for many births and then received Your Grace. If this person, who does not obey Your instructions, is also going to get it, then why should we have strived so hard to conform to Your laws?"

So God says, "I do not break My laws. Just as you need to follow the laws of nature while you live, I too have My laws, in accordance with which I work. If you go to any country, the laws of that country will be applicable to you. Similarly, you have come in My world, and My laws prevail here." What then is the condition for receiving Grace?

The Condition for God's Grace

God says that His eternal law is very simple: Those who surrender to Him will receive His Grace."

The Bhagavad Geeta states this law:

तमेव शरणं गच्छ सर्व भावेन भारत।
तत्प्रसादात् परां शान्तिं स्थानं प्राप्स्यसि शाश्वतम्।। (भगवद् गीता १८.६२)

tameva śharaṇaṁ gachchha sarva bhāvena bhārata
tatprasādāt parāṁ śhāntiṁ sthānaṁ prāpsyasi śhāśhvatam
(Bhagavad Geeta 18.62)

Shree Krishna says, "Arjun, surrender yourself to God. Then by His Grace, you will attain perfect peace and the Divine Abode." Let us now try to understand, what it mean to surrender to God.

The Nature of Surrender to God

Surrender has been defined in the Hari Bhakti Vilās, Bhakti Rasāmṛita Sindhu, the Vāyu Purāṇa, and the Ahirbudhni Sanhitā in the following manner:

आनुकूल्यस्य संकल्पः प्रतिकूल्यस्य वर्जनम्।
रक्षिष्यतीति विश्वासो गोप्तृत्वे वरणं तथा।
आत्मनिक्षेप कार्पण्ये षड्विधा शरणागतिः।। (हरि भक्ति विलास ११.६७६)

ānukūlyasya saṅkalpaḥ pratikūlyasya varjanam
rakṣhiṣhyatīti viśhvāso goptṛitve varaṇaṁ tathā
ātmanikṣhepa kārpaṇye ṣhaḍvidhā śharaṇāgatiḥ
(Hari Bhakti Vilāsa 11.676)

The above verse explains the six aspects of surrender to God:

1. To desire only in accordance with the desire of God. By nature, we are His servants, and the duty of a servant is to fulfill the desire of the master. So, as surrendered devotees of God, we must make our will conform to the will of God.

A dry leaf is surrendered to the wind. It does not complain whether the wind lifts it up, takes it forward or backward, or drops it to the ground. Similarly, we too must learn to be happy in the happiness of God.

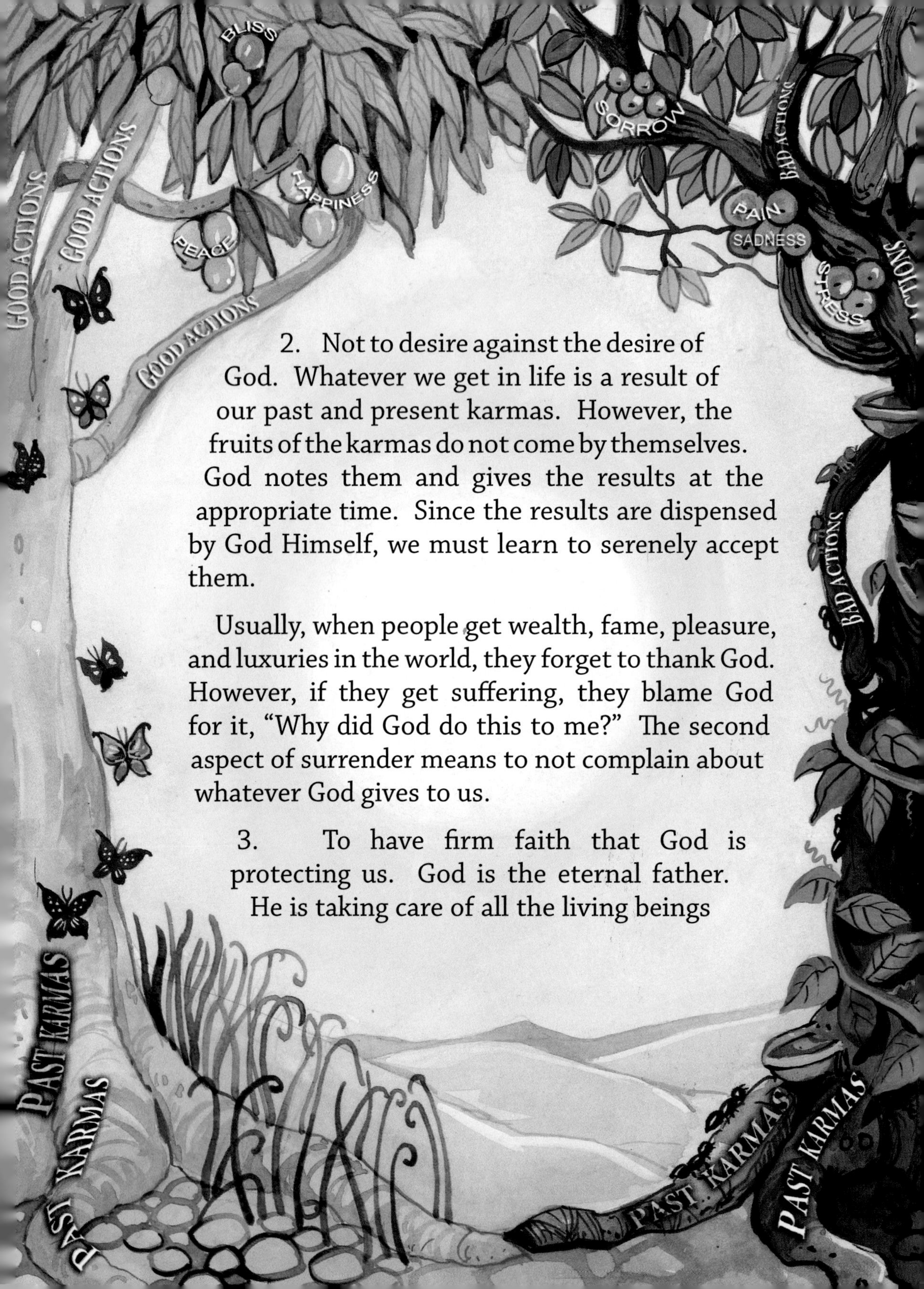

2. Not to desire against the desire of God. Whatever we get in life is a result of our past and present karmas. However, the fruits of the karmas do not come by themselves. God notes them and gives the results at the appropriate time. Since the results are dispensed by God Himself, we must learn to serenely accept them.

Usually, when people get wealth, fame, pleasure, and luxuries in the world, they forget to thank God. However, if they get suffering, they blame God for it, "Why did God do this to me?" The second aspect of surrender means to not complain about whatever God gives to us.

3. To have firm faith that God is protecting us. God is the eternal father. He is taking care of all the living beings

in creation. There are trillions of ants on the planet earth, and all of them need to eat regularly. Do you ever find that a few thousand ants in your garden have died of starvation? God ensures that they are all provided for. On the other hand, elephants eat mounds of food every day. God provides for them too. Even a worldly father cares and provides for his children. Why then should we doubt whether our eternal father, God, will take care of us or not? To have firm faith in His protection is the third aspect of surrender.

4. To keep an attitude of Gratitude towards God. We have received so many priceless gifts from the Lord. The earth that we walk upon, the sunlight with which we see, the air that we breathe and the water that we drink, are all given to us by God. In fact, it is because of Him that we exist; He has brought us to life and imparted consciousness in our soul. We are not paying Him any tax in return, but we must at least feel deeply indebted for all that He has given to us. This is the sentiment of gratitude.

The reverse of this is the sentiment of ungratefulness. For example, a father does so much for his child. The child is told to be grateful to his father for this. But the child responds, "Why should I be grateful? His father took care of him and he is taking care of me." This is ingratitude towards the worldly father. To be grateful towards God, our eternal Father, for all that He has given to us, is the fourth aspect of surrender.

5. To see everything we possess as belonging to God. This entire world has been created by God. It existed even before we were born, and will continue to exist even after we die. Hence, the true owner of everything is God alone. When we think something belongs to us, we forget the proprietorship of God.

Let us say that someone comes into your house when you are not at home. He wears your clothes, takes things out of your refrigerator, eats them, and sleeps on your bed. On returning, you ask indignantly, "What have you been doing in my house?"

He says, "I have not damaged anything. I have merely used everything properly. Why are you getting annoyed?"

You will reply, "You may not have destroyed anything, but it all belongs to me. If you use it without my permission, you are a thief."

Similarly, this world and everything that is in it belongs to God. To remember this, and give up our sense of proprietorship is the fifth aspect of surrender.

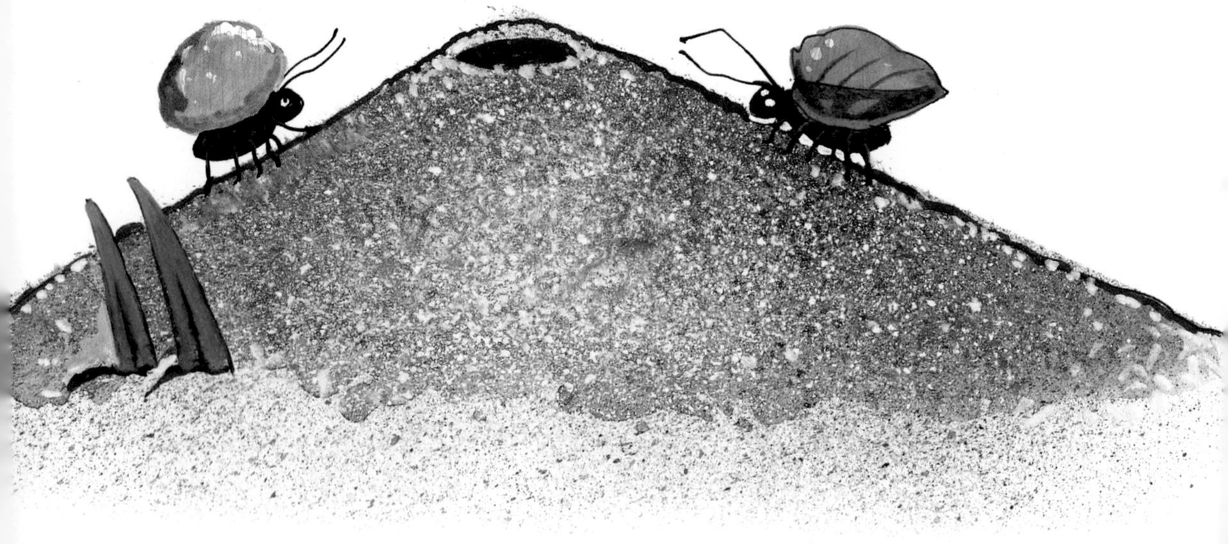

6. To give up the pride of having surrendered. If we become proud of the good deeds that we have done, the pride dirties our heart and undoes the good. That is why it is important to keep an attitude of humbleness: “If I was able to do something nice, it was only because God inspired my intellect in the right direction. Left to myself, I would never have been able to do it.” To keep such an attitude of humility is the sixth aspect of surrender.

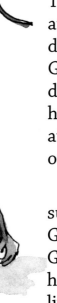

If we can perfect these six points of surrender in ourselves, we will fulfill God’s condition and He will bestow His Grace upon us. So, we now need to learn how to implement this surrender in our lives. For this, we will need the guidance of a Guru, which we shall discuss in the next chapter.卐

Chapter 8 The Spiritual Master

The Ignorance within Us

Since eternity, we are afflicted by the disease of ignorance. It is because of this lack of true knowledge, that we are unable to reach our goal in life. We want happiness, but we get misery; we want peace, but we experience conflict; we want to succeed, but we repeatedly experience failure. We all know that anger, greed, hatred, envy, pride, etc., are undesirable, and we want to get rid of them. But we do not know how to remove them from within us. If we did, we too would have been like the Buddha.

A quarrelsome person came to the Buddha and began heaping abuses upon him. The Buddha kept listening serenely to his offender. After an hour, the person got exhausted and became quiet. The Buddha told his disciples, "He has got tired. Give him something to eat and drink, so that he may begin again."

That person was astonished. He said, "Sir, are you made of wood or stone? Do you have no feelings? I abused you so much,

but you did not even complain!"

The Buddha said, "My dear fellow! If you give an object to someone, but that person does not take it, with whom does the object remain?"

"It remains with the person who gave it."

"Similarly, I did not accept all that you gave to me. So it is still with you."

Such behavior shows that the Buddha had finished the ignorance within him, and was seated in knowledge. However, we are far from that state as yet. We become infuriated if someone utters even one unpleasant sentence. Our anger, greed, envy, etc., are evidence of the ignorance within us. So we must strive to remove it to make our lives successful.

Understand the Scriptures from a Guru

How will we remove our ignorance within us? Even in the world, if we wish to learn Mathematics, Physics, or Geography, we do not do so on our own. We acquire knowledge of any subject through text books and a teacher. The text books contain the knowledge, but they are difficult to understand on our own. So along with the books, we take the help of a teacher as well.

Spiritual knowledge too, must be learnt from text books and a teacher. The Vedic scriptures are the text books that contain a vast treasure-house of Divine knowledge. But they are very intricate and complex. So we understand their meaning through a Guru. The Vedas say:

तद्विज्ञानार्थं स गुरुमेवाभिगच्छेत् समित्पाणिः श्रोत्रियं ब्रह्मनिष्ठम्।।
(मुण्डकोपनिषद् १.२.१२)

tadvigyānārthaṁ sa gurumevābhigachchhet samitpāṇiḥ śhrotriyaṁ brahmaniṣhṭham (Muṇḍakopanishad 1.2.12)

"Seek a God-realized Saint, who is well versed in the knowledge of the scriptures, and learn the spiritual secrets from him."

The Bhagavad Geeta states:

तद्विद्धि प्रणिपातेन परिप्रश्नेन सेवया।
उपदेक्ष्यन्ति ते ज्ञानं ज्ञानिनस्तत्त्वदर्शिनः।। (भगवद् गीता ४.३४)

tadviddhi praṇipātena paripraśhnena sevayā
upadekṣhyanti te gyānaṁ gyāninastattvadarśhinaḥ
(Bhagavad Geeta 4.34)

Shree Krishna says: "To get knowledge of God, approach a Guru. Surrender unto Him, serve Him with faith, and enquire submissively from Him. He will impart Divine knowledge unto you because He has realized the Truth."

The Qualifications of a Guru

The word "guru" has been adopted into the English language, and has come to mean "expert in the field". Nowadays, it is common to call an expert as a Management guru, or an Economics guru, etc. However, here we are talking about a Guru in the spiritual realm. Whom can we call a true Guru?

The Vedas describe two qualifications that the Guru must possess. The first qualification is that he must be *śhrotriya*, or a knower of the scriptures. He must be well-versed in scriptural knowledge, and have the ability to impart it to us.

The second qualification is that the Guru must be *brahm niṣhṭha*, or God-realized. Only one who is God-realized himself, can he help others to reach that state. This is common sense. We can give to others only what we possess for ourselves. Blind people cannot show others the path; illiterate people cannot teach others how to read; ignorant people cannot give others knowledge. Similarly, only one who has realized God can help others attain that state.

Thus, the Guru is one who is *śhrotriya brahm niṣṭha,* or accomplished in both—theoretical knowledge and practical realization. Such a Guru is called *Sadguru*, or one situated in the Truth.

The True Guru is Respected Like God

The True Guru is someone who has no personal desires of his own. He has merged his will with the will of God. Also, He is free from any pride and self-seeking. Such a *Sadguru* does nothing of his own accord. God becomes his guide and inspires his actions from within. Thus, the Guru becomes an instrument through whom God does His Divine work of elevating souls in the world. For such a true Guru, it is said:

गुरुर्ब्रह्मा गुरुर्विष्णुर्गुरुर्देवो महेश्वरः।
गुरुः साक्षात् परब्रह्म तस्मै श्री गुरवे नमः।।

gururbrahmā gururviṣhṇurgururdevo maheśhvaraḥ
guruḥ sākṣhāt parabrahma tasmai śhrī gurave namaḥ

"Respect your Guru as you would respect God. Look upon him as the form of Brahma, Vishnu, and Shankar."

Follow the Instructions of the Guru

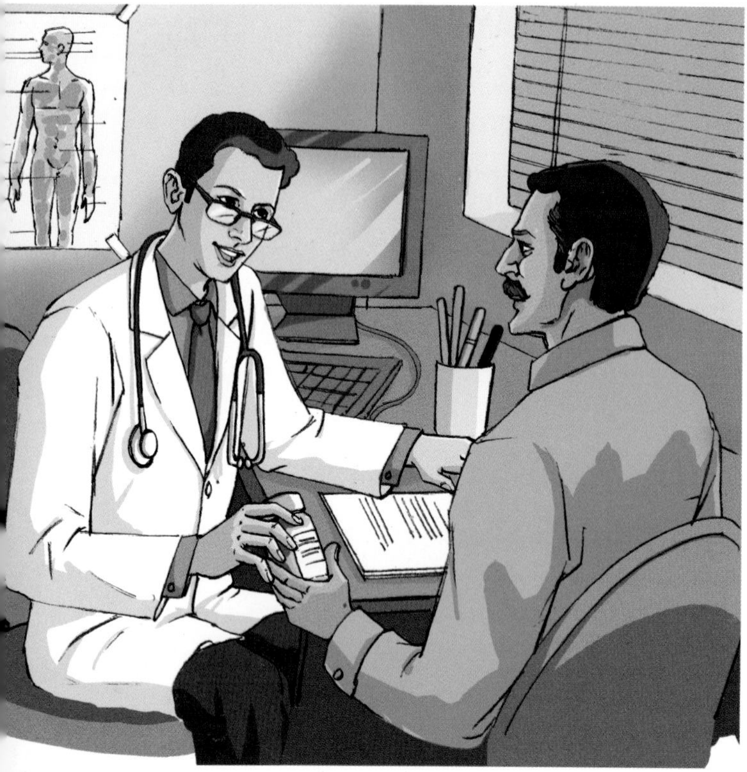

Once we find a God-realized Guru, we must then follow His instructions, if we wish to benefit from him. This is just as when we are sick, we go to a doctor. We explain our symptoms to the doctor. Beyond that, we do not use our intellect. The doctor understands our problem and then tells us the remedy. "Take two tablespoons of this medicine thrice a day for one month, and you will become all right." We follow the doctor's instructions and get cured.

Now suppose we used our intellect, "The doctor has told me to take a little medicine everyday for one month. Let me take all of it today, so that I may be cured in one day itself." If we were to do that, the doctor would not be able to cure us. Similarly, the Guru can only cure us from the disease of ignorance, if we follow his instructions. So we must first learn the secrets of the scriptures from a true Guru, and then act in accordance with them, to surrender to God.卐

Chapter 9

The Importance of the Mind

Personality is Fashioned by Thoughts

From the Guru, we will learn the process for purifying the mind, for surrender to God. This mind is a subtle machine within us that keeps creating thoughts. These thoughts are like waves. There are innumerable waves in the atmosphere. You cannot see them, but they do exist. Take a radio set and turn the frequency knob. One after another, you will keep picking up radio stations. This implies that multiple waves exist in the atmosphere. If you receive a call or an SMS on the mobile phone, it is through waves in the atmosphere. Similarly, our thoughts are also waves created by the mind.

The thoughts that we harbor affect our personality. You look at someone and say, "He seems like an angry fellow." The thoughts of anger that the person dwelled upon, chiseled his face to give him an angry look. You look at someone else and say, "She seems to be very simple and trustworthy." Her thoughts of simplicity, honesty, and integrity created a corresponding look on her face.

The mind is a machine that continuously generates thoughts. The quality of our thoughts is very important in determining our success in life. If someone thinks pure, noble, beautiful, serene, and calm thoughts, that person's life becomes blessed. Such a person naturally attracts good things in life. If someone thinks selfish, violent, dishonest, and impure thoughts, that person attracts misfortune in life. Hence, for achieving greatness and for realizing God, we must learn to harbor good thoughts in our mind.

Cultivate the Garden of Your Mind

If you had a garden at home, you would tend to it regularly. You would put fertilizer in the soil. You would sow the proper seeds and water the plants daily. At the same time, you would be careful to weed out the wild grass, else it would grow faster than the plants and choke them out. If you worked hard in tending your garden, it would reward you with luscious fruits and beautiful flowers. However, if you left it to grow wild, it would be overrun by weeds, and become unsightly and disgustful.

The mind too is like a garden given to us by God. The fertile soil of our mind has the potential of generating inspiring thoughts, lofty ideas, and noble feelings. But for this, we need to tend to it carefully, planting in it elevating thoughts, and pulling out the weeds of poisonous feeling. The mind will then reward us with a noble, sterling, and heroic character that will help us accomplish great things in life. People who achieved greatness, did so by cultivating the mind.

The Saint Shankaracharya posed the question: *jagat jitaṁ kena?* "Who shall conquer this world?" The wise answer he gave was: *mano hī yena*. One who conquers his or her own mind, not one who has superior weapons or greater wealth. When someone reins in and elevates the mind, that person's thoughts and ideas become so inspiring, that they influence the whole world.

The average person's mind is not under control. Students often experience this, when they sit in front of the textbook to read. They find their mind wandering all over the world. Scientists estimate that we use only three percent of our mental and intellectual potential. The rest is dissipated because of lack of focus of the mind.

You Are Where Your Mind Is

Our experience of happiness and distress in life is all a product of our mind. Harboring positive thoughts, such as love, sacrifice, admiration, kindness, generosity, etc., makes us happy. Holding negative thoughts, such as hatred, fear, anxiety, resentment, jealousy, etc., makes us miserable. Thus, our experience of happiness and distress is not dependent upon our external situation, but upon the state of the mind. Even while living

in hellish circumstances, a trained mind can make us experience heavenly bliss. On the other hand, even whilst living amidst heavenly luxuries, an uncontrolled mind can make us experience hellish miseries. Hence, effectively, we are where our mind is.

The *Purāṇas* relate a story in this regard. There were two brothers, Tavrit and Suvrit. They

were walking from their house to the temple, which was two hours away, to attend a discourse on the Shreemad Bhagavatam. On the way, they got caught in a rainstorm. They ran for shelter to the nearest building. Entering it, they realized that it was a sinful place, where people engaged in vulgar dancing and drinking.

The elder brother, Tavrit, was outraged. "How awful!" he said, "Let us get out of this place and reach the temple."

His younger brother, Suvrit, tried to pacify him. "It is raining heavily outside. What is the harm in remaining here until the rain ceases? They are not forcing us to join them in their sinful activities."

Tavrit was adamant and walked out of the building in a huff. He got drenched in the rain for one-and-a-half hours, but reached the temple. There he sat and heard Punditji's discourse on the Shreemad Bhagavatam with his ears. However, in his mind, he began thinking, "This is so boring. I made a mistake by coming here. My brother must be really enjoying himself with the wine, song, and dance."

Suvrit, on the other hand, was repenting. "This place is so vulgar," he thought. "I made a mistake by remaining here. I too should have braved the rain, like Tavrit, and I would have gotten to hear the holy message of the Shreemad Bhagavatam instead of having to watch this."

When the rain finally subsided, both got out and began walking in each other's direction. As soon as they met, lightning fell on them and they died. The *Purāṇas* say that *Yamdoots*, or the servants of Yamraj, the God of death, came to take Tavrit, and *Vishnudoots*, or the servants of Lord Vishnu came to take Suvrit.

"You seem to have gotten the wrong name," said Tavrit. "I was sitting in the temple. It was my brother who was at the Inn."

"We have made no mistake," replied the *Vishnudoots*. "You were physically at the temple but mentally at the Inn. While Suvrit was physically at the Inn, but mentally at the temple." Thus, God gives us the fruits in accordance to where we keep our mind.

Hence, the Pañchadaśhī states:

मन एव मनुष्याणां कारणं बन्ध मोक्षयोः। (पँचदशी)

mana eva manuṣhyāṇāṁ kāraṇaṁ bandha mokṣhayoḥ
(Pañchadaśhī)

"Liberation and bondage in Maya is decided by the condition of the mind." If it is attached to the world, it results in bondage, and the soul continues to rotate in the cycle of life and death. But if the mind is attached to God, it results in liberation from the material realm.

The Three Modes of Material Nature

Our mind is made from Maya, or the material energy. This Maya consists of three modes: *sattva guṇa*, or the mode of goodness, *rajo guṇa*, or the mode of passion, and *tamo guṇa*, or the mode of ignorance. These three modes are in Maya, and they exist in our mind as well. Depending upon our environment and where we focus our thoughts, one of the *guṇas* becomes prominent and our mind takes on that quality.

If *sattva guṇa* dominates, one becomes peaceful, contented, generous, kind, helpful, and serene. When *rajo guṇa* gains prominence, one becomes passionate, agitated, ambitious, envious of others' success, and desirous for sense pleasures. When *tamo guṇa* becomes prominent, one is overcome by sleep, laziness, hatred, anger, resentment, violence, and doubt.

For example, let us suppose you are sitting in your reading room, engaged in study. There is no worldly disturbance and your mind becomes *sāttvic*. After finishing your study, you sit in your drawing room and switch on the television. Seeing all the imagery makes your mind *rājasic*, and increases your hankering for sense pleasures. While you are watching your favorite channel, your sister comes and changes the channel to her liking. This disturbance causes *tamo guṇa* to develop in your mind, and you are filled with anger. In this way, our mind sways between the three *guṇas*, and takes on the corresponding qualities.

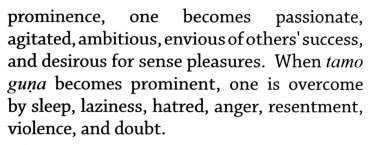

How to Control the Mind

Since the mind is made from the material energy, it can only be controlled if we conquer Maya. However, this Maya is an energy of God. If someone conquers Maya, it means that person has conquered God Himself. No one can conquer God, and hence, no one can conquer Maya either. Thus, we see that people strive in various ways to tame their mind, but

nothing seems to work, for none of these techniques can defeat Maya. There is only one technique that will work, and that is to surrender the mind to God.

Let us say, you wish to meet your friend, and reach the gate of his house. He has a board on his fence, "Beware of dog". His pet Alsatian is standing in his lawn and that fierce creature growls at you menacingly. You decide to try the back gate and go around the fence. However, the Alsatian comes around too and snarls furiously, conveying the message, "I dare you to step into this house."

When you have no other option, you call out to your friend. He steps out of his door and sees his dog troubling you. He calls out, "No, Tommy! Come and sit here." The dog is immediately pacified and comes and sits by his side.

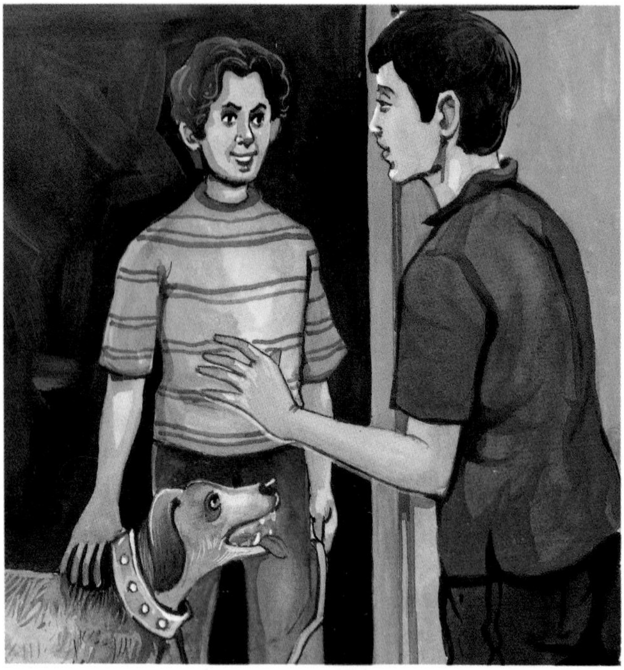

Now, you open the gate and walk fearlessly inside.

Similarly, the material energy is troubling us, but it is subservient to God. The way to overcome it is to surrender to Him. Shree Krishna says in the Bhagavad Geeta:

दैवी ह्येषा गुणमयी मम माया दुरत्यया।
मामेव ये प्रपद्यन्ते मायामेतां तरन्ति ते।। (भगवद् गीता ७.१४)

daivī hyeṣhā guṇamayī mama māyā duratyayā
māmeva ye prapadyante māyāmetāṁ taranti te (Geeta 7.14)

"This material energy of Mine is very difficult to overcome. But, when one submits to Me, I indicate to Maya to release that person."

The mind is thus to be conquered by surrendering it to God. For accomplishing this, the Vedas give various paths, which we will discuss next.

Chapter 10 The Path of Karm

The Three Paths to God-realization

A farmer wanted to dig a well in his new property. He dug three feet in one place, and exclaimed, "I am not getting any water here. Let me dig elsewhere." He dug four feet in the next place and said, "There is a rock bed here. I will try elsewhere." In the third place, he dug two feet and stopped, saying, "All I am getting here is pebbles. There is no water in this place." In this way the farmer dug fifty wells but he did not get water anywhere. However, if he had selected the right place and then continued to dig for a few hundred feet, he would definitely have reached water. Similarly, if we are confused about the path to God-realization, we will keep trying different ways and reach nowhere. Hence, it is important to have a clear knowledge about the paths to God.

There is a name for God in the Vedas: *Sat-chit-ānand*. These three, *sat, chit,* and *ānand* refer to three energies of God. The nature of *sat* is action, or *Karm*. The nature of *chit* is knowledge, or *Gyān*. And the nature of *ānand* is devotion, or *Bhakti*. Hence, God has three aspects to His nature—*Karm, Gyān,* and *Bhakti*.

We tiny souls are small parts of God, and hence we too have the same three aspects to our nature, although smaller in measure. This is just as a drop of water has the qualities of the ocean. The three aspects of our nature are *Karm*, or work, *Gyān*, or knowledge, and *Bhakti*, or devotion. Accordingly, the scriptures state three paths to God:

योगास्त्रयो मया प्रोक्ता नृणां श्रेयोविधित्सया।
ज्ञानं कर्म च भक्तिश्च नोपायोऽन्योऽस्ति कुत्रचित्।। (भागवतम् ११.२०.६)

yogāstrayo mayā proktā nṛiṇāṁ śhreyovidhitsayā
gyānaṁ karma cha bhaktiśhcha nopāyo 'nyo 'sti kutrachit
(Shreemad Bhagavatam 11.20.6)

"There are three paths to reach God—*Karm, Gyān,* and *Bhakti*. No other way exists." We will now consider these paths, one by one. First, let us discuss the path of *Karm*.

Duties in Life

Whoever we are, we always have duties to fulfill. These duties ensure that we learn to regulate our mind and intellect. Without them, humans would descend to the level of beasts. Hinduism divides these duties into two parts—spiritual duties and social duties:

Spiritual duties: These are our duties towards God, Who is our eternal Father, Mother, Friend, and Well-wisher.

Performing these is called *Bhakti*, or devotion, and results in the purification of the mind and the attainment of God.

The spiritual duties, or *Bhakti*, are the eternal principles that always remain the same, and which we have been discussing in the previous chapters. They are also called *par dharm*, or the spiritual aspect of religion.

Social duties: These are the duties we have towards our parents, friends and relatives, the society we live in, the nation of which we are citizens, etc. These duties have been described in the Vedas and are called *Karm*. They do not result in God-realization. However, fulfilling these duties ensures that we act in a responsible manner, and contribute towards the wellbeing and harmony of society.

The social duties, or *Karm*, are based on our occupation and position in life. And they may change from time to time, depending upon the nature of society, etc. They are also called *apar dharm*, or the material aspect of religion.

Karm or Social Duties

As mentioned earlier, the social duties mentioned in Vedas are called *Karm*. These are in accordance with one's *āśhram* (stage in life) and *varṇa* (occupation). They helped society function in a harmonious manner, giving everyone an opportunity to do their duties according to their natures and gradually perfect their lives to reach God-realization. Some of these duties are not relevant today since the nature of society has changed. But they helped organize Hindu society thousands of years ago, while humans in the western world were still living in forests.

In this *varṇāśhram* system, the duties were according to one's nature and occupation, not according to birth. However, with the passage of time, the system got degraded and the classifications became based on birth. This was a wrong interpretation of what was mentioned in the Vedas. However, when the British ruled India, they highlighted the social practice, and called it "caste system". They publicized it so much that even today in USA, if the discussion of Hinduism comes up, the only thing many people know about it is the caste system. They are not aware of the sublime knowledge of the science of God realization that exists in Hinduism, which has no comparison anywhere in the world.

It is thus necessary to clarify that the *varṇāśhram* system was not a part of the spiritual principles of Hinduism. It was a set of social duties described in Hinduism thousands of years ago, when civilization in the western world had not even begun. It got distorted with time, but that was a social defect and Hinduism cannot be blamed for it. This is just as slavery existed in the western world until two hundred years ago, but we do not blame Christianity, Islam, or Judaism for this social practice. In fact, even until the 1960s, discrimination on the basis of skin color existed in USA. This was a social ill but we do not find fault Christianity for it. Similarly, the *varṇāśhram* system got distorted as a social ill in India, but it is wrong to blame Hinduism for it.

Karmakāṇḍ—The Ritualistic Ceremonies

A part of the social duties is *Karmakāṇḍ*, or the ritualistic ceremonies, that help purify the mind. Very few people have so much of love for God that they can simply sit and meditate upon Him. Most people need some rituals or external ceremonial procedures to help them engage the mind positively. The Vedas describe such *Karmakāṇḍ*, or ceremonial procedures. Some of them are mentioned below:

***Dīpam*, or lighting of the lamp.** At the beginning of most Hindu ceremonies, a lamp is lit, which is often kept lighted throughout the ceremony. The light of the lamp is symbolic of the knowledge of God, which removes the darkness of ignorance within our hearts.

Prayer room and Altar. Most Indian homes have a prayer room and an altar, on which images of God and the Guru are placed. These help us remember that God is the actual Master and owner of the house. He is the Head of the family. Also, the environment in the prayer room helps develop sacred thoughts when we sit there for worship, meditation, and devotional singing.

***Ārati*, or ceremony of lights.** With great faith and reverence, a lamp is waved around the deity, or image of God. This helps develop the spirit of glorifying the Lord with loving remembrance. Hence it is often accompanied with the ringing of bells and the chanting of songs. As the lamp goes around illuminating the different parts of the deity, it helps focus the mind on the image of God. It is akin to open-eyed meditation on the beauty of God. After the *ārati*, the lamp is taken around to the devotees. They place their hands over the flame and then put their hands on their eyes and head. This is a symbolic way of receiving the blessings and *śhakti* (energy) of the Deities.

***Tilak*, or holy marks.** God resides within everyone's heart, and hence the body is a temple of God. Holy marks are applied on the body to remind us that it is the abode of God, and hence it is sacred. The *Tilak* is a symbol of God, and reminds us of Him.

***Pradakṣhiṇā*, or going around the deity in the temple.** It is a way of showing respect to the deity. It also symbolizes that we will try to keep the Lord as the center of our life as we go about our daily duties.

<u>Prasād.</u> In Hinduism, food is first offered to God and later taken as *prasād*, or the Grace of God. Since God is everywhere, if we offer to Him with love, He accepts. We then take the food as His remnants. This creates a Divine attitude within us towards the food we eat.

***<u>Upavās</u>*, <u>or fasting.</u>** Every day, a lot of time and energy is spent in procuring, cooking, and eating food. On certain days, fasts are suggested, to reduce the emphasis on eating and to dedicate that time to prayer and worship. Also, once in a while, eating only simple food, or not eating at all, gives relief to the digestive system and helps keep it healthy.

<u>Namaste.</u> This is a very beautiful and sacred way of greeting each other with respect and humility. *Namaste* means "I bow to you." It is done with folded hands in front of the chest, to indicate reverence, and bowing of the head, to display humbleness.

<u>Bowing down before elders or touching their feet.</u> In Hinduism, parents and elders are respected by touching their feet or bowing down before them. In turn, the elders raise their hand or place it on our head in blessing. This is done daily when we meet them, and particularly, on special occasions. Touching the feet is a way of acknowledging the greatness of the other person. The tradition strengthens the family bonds, preserves the humbleness of the youngsters, and ensures that they get the guidance and blessings of the seniors.

Not touching paper, books, and people with the feet. In the Indian culture, all knowledge, both material and spiritual—is considered Divine. So it must be treated with respect. People too are Divine parts of God. Hence, touching books or people with the feet is considered disrespectful.

There are many more rituals and their essence is to develop love and respect for God and His world within our minds.

Karmyog

Karm, or social duties, help in regulating the mind, and elevating it to the mode of goodness. However, they cannot take us beyond Maya, to meet God. So for those who are eager for God-realization, we have the system of *Karmyog*. *Karm* means "work" and *yog* means "to unite with God". *Karmyog* teaches us how to reach God while performing our worldly duties.

The principle of *Karmyog* is explained in the Bhagavad Geeta:

सर्वेषु कालेषु मामनुस्मर युध्य च। (भगवद् गीता ८.७)

sarveṣhu kāleṣhu māmanusmara yudhya cha (Geeta 8.7)

Shree Krishna says to Arjun, "Do your duty, but at the same time, always remember Me." Saints give the example of a cow; it grazes grass in the fields all day long. But its mind remains in its calf that is in the cowshed.

At present, we remember God sometimes, as when we go to the temple. But we forget that this whole world is a temple of God and He is present wherever we go. In *Karmyog*, we practice to feel the presence of God always with us as our Protector and Witness. And then, we learn to perform every work for His pleasure. When we work with this attitude, we naturally put in our best efforts. However, if the results are unfavorable, we do not feel stressed because they are not for our sake. For example, we will study hard for the pleasure of God, but if the results are not as we hoped, we will calmly accept them as the will of God. Shree Krishna explains this art of work in the Bhagavad Geeta:

कर्मण्येवाधिकारस्ते मा फलेषु कदाचन। (भगवद् गीता २.४७)

karmaṇyevādhikāraste mā phaleṣhu kadāchana (Geeta 2.47)

"You have the right to work, but do not be attached to the fruits of your actions."

In this way, a *Karmyogī* reaches God through devotion, while fulfilling the social duties as well. 卐

Chapter 11 The Path of *Gyān*

The Power of Knowledge

Knowledge gives great power, and the person with superior knowledge can accomplish in a few days what would take others years to achieve. If a small wire in an airplane gets disconnected, the airplane is unable to take off from the ground. Hundreds of people work at the airport, but they cannot do anything about it, and the airplane worth millions of dollars remains grounded. One aero-mechanic comes, reconnects the wire, and the airplane is ready to fly again. What did the aero-mechanic have that others did not? He possessed superior knowledge about the plane's machinery and functioning.

In the spiritual realm too, knowledge carries the same kind of power. Social scientists say that as civilization is evolving, it has moved from an agricultural-based society, to a manufacturing-based society, and presently it is moving towards a knowledge-

DELHI AIRPORT

based society. Success in any enterprise is becoming increasingly dependent upon the quality of knowledge we possess. Amazingly, 5000 years ago, Shree Krishna had glorified the power of knowledge in the Bhagavad Geeta. He told Arjun:

न हि ज्ञानेन सदृशं पवित्रमिह विद्यते। (भगवद् गीता ४.३८)

na hi gyānena sadṛiśhaṁ pavitramiha vidyate (Geeta 4.38)

"There is nothing as pure in this world as true knowledge." In the Hindu tradition, we are fortunate to have a vast treasure-house of knowledge available in the Vedic scriptures.

Praise for Indian Scriptures by Western Scholars

The Vedic scriptures have been extolled by all the Western scholars, whoever read them. These philosophers and intellectuals had this to say about the Vedic texts:

"I owed a magnificent day to the Bhagavad Geeta, the first amongst books. It was as if an empire spoke to me; nothing small or unworthy, but large, serene, and consistent; the voice of an old intelligence, which in another age and climate, had pondered and disposed that same questions which exercise us." Ralph Waldo Emerson, Philosopher (1803-1882).

"In the morning, I bathe my intellect in the stupendous and cosmogonal philosophy of the Bhagavad Geeta, in comparison to which our modern world and its literature seems puny and trivial." Henry David Thoreau, American Philosopher and Naturalist (1817-1862).

"Whenever I have read any part of the Vedas, I have felt that a Divine light illuminated me. In the great teaching of the Vedas, there is no touch of sectarianism. When I am at it, I feel that

I am under the spangled heavens of a summer night." Henry David Thoreau, American Writer, Philosopher, and Naturalist (1817 to 1862).

"When we read the philosophical monuments of the East, above all, those of India, we discover in them, many truths so highly elevated in contrast to which the European genius has stopped, that we are constrained to bend our knees before the philosophy of India." Victor Cousin, French philosopher (1792-1867)

Albert Einstein

"When I read the Bhagavad Geeta, and reflect about how God created this universe, everything else seems so superfluous. We owe a lot to the Indians, who taught us how to count, without which no scientific discovery would have been possible. " Albert Einstein, American Scientist (1879-1955).

"There is nothing in this world as elevating as the Upanishads. They have been the solace of my life and they shall be the solace of my death." Arthur Schopenhauer, German philosopher (1788 to 1860).

"If these words of Schopenhauer require any confirmation, I shall gladly give it as the result of my lifelong study of the Vedic scriptures." Professor Max Muller, German Orientalist, considered as the father of comparative religion (1823 to 1900).

"Eternal philosophical truth has seldom found a more striking and decisive expression than in the emancipating knowledge of the philosophy of the Upanishads." Paul Deussen, German Orientalist, Sanskrit scholar, and author of "The System of Vedanta" (1845 to 1919).

"Access to the Vedas is the greatest privilege this century may claim over previous centuries." J Robert Oppenheimer, American Nuclear Physicist (1904-1957).

Aldous Huxley

"The Bhagavad Geeta is one of the clearest and most comprehensive summaries of the perennial philosophy ever to have been done. Hence its enduring value, not only for the Indians, but also for all mankind. It is perhaps the most systematic statement of the perennial philosophy." Aldous Huxley, English Writer (1894-1963)

Theoretical and Realized Knowledge

While knowledge has been given such a high place in Hinduism, it has also been criticized. The *Īśhopaniṣhad* states:

अन्धं तमः प्रविशन्ति येऽविद्यामुपासते।
ततो भूय इव ते तमो य उ विद्यायाꣳ रताः।। (ईशोपनिषद्)

andhaṁ tamaḥ praviśhanti ye 'vidyāmupāsate
tato bhūya iva te tamo ya u vidyāyāṁ ratāḥ (Īśhopaniṣhad)

"Those who do not cultivate knowledge attain darkness. But those who go by the path of knowledge, attain an even greater darkness." Isn't that surprising! If knowledge is illuminating, how can it lead to darkness?

This is so because there are two kinds of knowledge—theoretical knowledge and practical knowledge. For example, let us say that a lady has learnt by heart, all the recipes in her cookbook, but has never even entered the kitchen in her life. Undoubtedly she possesses knowledge of cooking, but it is merely theoretical knowledge. Another woman has been cooking for the last sixty years, and has experience of all its intricacies. She possesses practical knowledge of cooking. Such knowledge is far superior to mere bookish knowledge.

A person had a pet parrot. Out of selfless love for his pet, he decided to free it from the cage. Before that, he taught it to say,

"O Parrot! Do not sit on the net, else the hunter will capture you and take you away."

The parrot learnt to repeat the sentence perfectly, "O Parrot! Do not sit on the net, else the hunter will capture you and take you away." The owner thought that its parrot had become knowledgeable and would be able to take care of itself. He released it from the cage, to fly into the sky.

The parrot flew to the forest. There a hunter had spread his net to catch birds. The parrot sat on the net and kept saying, "O Parrot! Do not sit on the net, else the hunter will capture you and take you away."

The hunter came and caught the bird in his net. He was carrying it away, but the unfortunate parrot that was caught in the net was still saying, "O Parrot! Do not sit on the net, else the hunter will capture you and take you away." What was the use of such knowledge?

Similarly, in the spiritual realm,

theoretical knowledge is that where one has read, or even memorized the scriptures, but has never done *sādhanā*, or spiritual practice. On the other hand, knowledge becomes practical realization when one actually surrenders to God, and by His Grace, gets experience for oneself.

Mere theoretical knowledge, which is without experience, leads to the pride of learning. Proud people think they know a lot, but their practical life does not reflect their knowledge. Hence, the Vedas say that instead of taking them upwards in life, such knowledge pulls them down. It is such empty and hollow learning that is criticized by the scriptures.

Practical realization makes a person humble because it makes one aware of his or her defects, and how much further one needs to go. Such knowledge has been praised in the scriptures. Thus, we must not only acquire the theoretical knowledge of the scriptures, but we must also practically apply it in our lives.

Gyānyog

Gyānyog is a spiritual path where the goal is to know the "self", or the soul. The *Gyānyogī* strives to attain knowledge of the self, and to be practically situated on that platform. This requires analyzing that one is not the body, senses, mind, intellect, and ego. The knowledge is first understood theoretically by hearing from the Guru and the scriptures. Then, one repeatedly meditates on this knowledge and tries to realize it practically.

In this manner, material desires related to the body slowly diminish. Finally, one gains insight into the nature of the self. The "self", or soul, is a tiny part of God.

चिन्मात्रं श्री हरेरंशं सूक्ष्ममक्षरमव्ययम्।। (वेद)

chinmātraṁ śhrī hareranśhaṁ sūkṣhmamakṣharamavyayam
(Vedas)

अँशो नाना व्यपदेशात्। (वेदान्त दर्शन २.३.४१)

anśho nānā vyapadeśhāt (Vedānta Darśhana 2.3.41)

ममैवांशो जीवलाके जीवभूतः सनातनः। (भगवद् गीता १५.७)

mamaivānśho jīvaloke jīvabhūtaḥ sanātanaḥ (Geeta 15.7)

ईश्वर अँश जीव अविनासी। चेतन अमल सहज सुख रासी।। (रामायण)

īśhvara anśha jīva avināsī
chetana amala sahaja sukha rāsī (Ramayan)

All these verses state that the soul is a tiny part of God. Knowledge of the self is called *ātma gyān*, while knowledge of God is called *Brahm gyān*. *Gyānyog* leads to *ātma gyān*, but as was stated earlier, knowledge of God, or *Brahm gyān*, cannot be attained by self-effort. It requires the Grace of God.

Hence, *Gyānyog* is incomplete until we surrender to God, and engage in His devotion. The *gyānī* needs to do *Bhakti* to attract the Grace of God, and complete the journey to God-realization.

Gyānyog is very difficult

Even though the *gyānī* finally attains God by doing *Bhakti*, it is a very difficult path. This is because the *gyānī* travels a major part of the journey merely by self effort, without the Grace of God.

Understand this by comparing a baby kitten and a baby monkey. The kitten is tiny in size and delicate in build. Yet, if it is to be moved from one place to another, it does not need to worry. Its mother holds the kitten with her mouth and carries it around. On the other hand, the baby monkey has to clasp onto her mother herself. The mother is not responsible for holding the baby monkey, while she jumps from one branch of the tree to another.

The path of *Gyānyog* is like that of the baby monkey, while the experience of the path of *Bhakti yog* is like that of the kitten. The *Gyānyogī* strives only by self-effort, without the Grace of God, and thus, every obstacle becomes formidable to overcome. But the *Bhakti yogī* surrenders to God from the beginning, and by the Grace of God, is easily able to cross over material obstacles to reach God.

Aṣhṭāṅg yog

This is a variation of *Gyānyog*. It aims to control the mind by physical means, and reach the state of *ātma gyān*. The procedure consists of eight steps. Hence, it is called *Aṣhṭāṅg yog*, or the eight-fold system. These steps help to gradually prepare the body and regulate the mind and senses, by following codes of conduct, practicing physical postures, breathing exercises, meditational techniques, etc.

The third step amongst these is *Āsan*. This has become famous all over the world as "Yoga". The western world has picked out the part of the eight-fold system that has to do with the physical postures, and it is practiced for good health, beauty, anti-aging, alternative healing, etc. It is considered fashionable nowadays to do Yoga, and scores of Yoga studios have opened in every city of the world. These physical *Yogāsans* are undoubtedly highly beneficial for physical health, but the spiritual aspect is often ignored.

The system of *Aṣhṭāṅg yog* helps develop the personality at the physical, mental, intellectual, and spiritual levels. However, it has one deficiency. It is based on self-effort, which is insufficient to control the mind, without the Grace of God. When we add *Bhakti* to it, that leads to true Yog, or union with God. The system of "Jagadguru Kripaluji Yog" teaches a perfect blend of the yogic techniques with *Bhakti*.

The Shreemad Bhagavatam states:

तत्कर्म हरितोषं यत्सा विद्या तन्मतिर्यया।। (श्रीमद् भागवतम् ४.२९.४९)

tatkarma haritoṣhaṁ yatsā vidyā tanmatiryayā
(Shreemad Bhagavatam 4.29.49)

"True knowledge is that which increases our love for God. True *Karm* is that which is done in devotion to God." In this way, every path needs the help of *Bhakti* for reaching the goal of God-realization.

We have seen how *Bhakti* is essential for success in any path. So let us now consider the nature of *Bhakti*, or Divine Love.

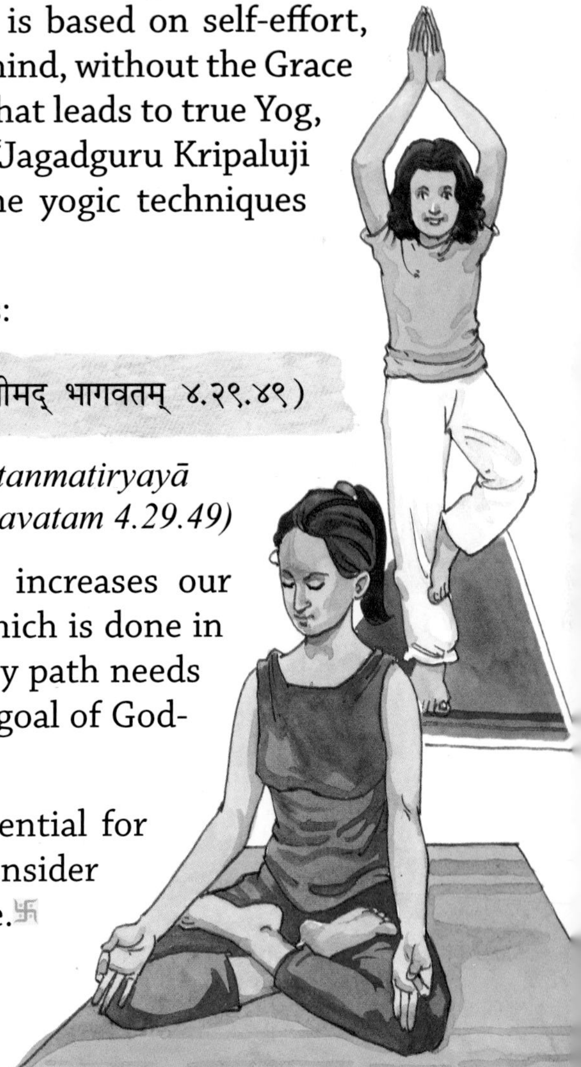

Chapter 12 The Path of Bhakti

Bhakti is Essential to Attain God

We have seen how for God-realization, *Bhakti* is essential in every path. The *Karmyogī* does *Bhakti* along with *Karm*, or worldly duties. The *Gyānyogī* and *Aṣhṭāṅg yogī* progress by their particular *sādhanā* path. However, at the end, they too need to do *Bhakti*, to attract the Grace of God, and reach the final destination. The scriptures state very categorically, that without *Bhakti*, no one can attain God.

भक्तिरेवैनं नयति भक्तिरेवैनं पश्यति।। (माठर श्रुति)

bhaktirevainaṁ nayati bhaktirevainaṁ paśhyati (Māṭhara Śhruti)

भक्त्याहमेकया ग्राह्यः श्रद्धयाऽऽत्मा प्रियः सताम्।
(श्रीमद् भागवतम् ११.१४.२१)

bhaktyāhamekayā grāhyaḥ śhraddhayātmā priyaḥ satām
(Shreemad Bhagavatam 11.14.21)

पुरुषः स परः पार्थ भक्त्या लभ्यस्त्वनन्यया। (भगवद् गीता ८.२२)

puruṣhaḥ sa paraḥ pārtha bhaktyā labhyastvananyayā
(Bhagavad Geeta 8.22)

भक्त्या त्वनन्यया शक्य अहमेवंविधोऽर्जुन। (भगवद् गीता ११.५४)

bhaktyā tvananyayā śhakya ahamevaṁvidho 'rjuna
(Bhagavad Geeta 11.54)

मिलहिं न रघुपति बिनु अनुरागा। किएँ योग तप ज्ञान विरागा।।

milahiñ na raghupati binu anurāgā, kiyeñ yoga tapa gyāna virāgā
(Ramayan)

All the above verses affirm that God is attained by Love alone. The essence of religion is to learn to Love God.

Devotion to God is the Nature of the Soul

Your hand is a part of your body, and the natural duty of the hand is to serve the body. It carries food to the mouth and feeds the body. In doing so, the hand automatically receives the nourishment, blood, and oxygen it needs for its own survival. The hand does not need to take care of itself separately. In caring for whatever it is a part of, its self-interest is automatically provided for.

Let us say, the hand refuses to serve the body, and says, "I have had enough! All my life has passed by in serving this repulsive body. No more now! Cut me away from it, I will take care of myself." Do you think the hand will be able to survive on its own? Definitely not! Its self-interest lies in serving what it is a part of.

The soul too, is an integral part of God. Hence, the natural duty of the soul is to serve God. By doing so, the soul automatically gets the Divine Knowledge, Love, and Bliss for which it has been hankering since eternity. Its self-interest is fulfilled by loving and serving God, of whom it is an integral part.

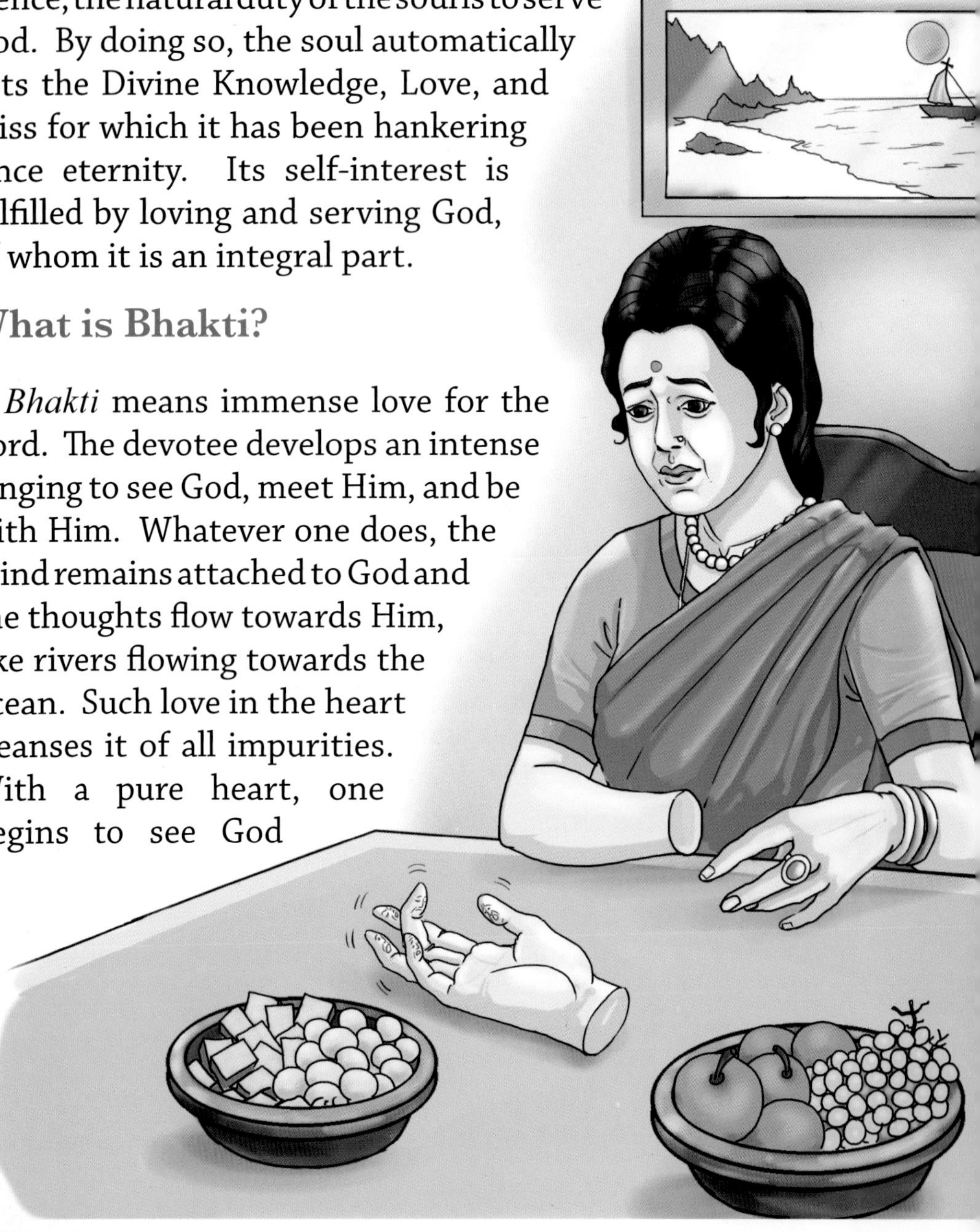

What is Bhakti?

Bhakti means immense love for the Lord. The devotee develops an intense longing to see God, meet Him, and be with Him. Whatever one does, the mind remains attached to God and the thoughts flow towards Him, like rivers flowing towards the ocean. Such love in the heart cleanses it of all impurities. With a pure heart, one begins to see God

in all living beings and in all things. As the thoughts become sublime, the devotee experiences the unlimited Divine Bliss of God and becomes fully satisfied.

A natural consequence of love for God is the desire to serve Him. The Sage Ved Vyas has defined *Bhakti* in this manner:

भज इत्येषवैधातुः सेवायां परिकीर्तितः।
तस्मात्सेवा बुधैः प्रोक्ता भक्तिः साधनभूयसी।। (गरुड़ पुराण)

bhaja ityeṣhavaidhātuḥ sevāyāṁ parikīrtitaḥ
tasmātsevā budhaiḥ proktā bhaktiḥ sādhanabhūyasī
(Garuḍa Purāṇa)

"The word *Bhakti* is made from the root *Bhaj*, which means 'to serve'. Hence, *Bhakti* is the desire to serve God." Even in the world, if we love someone, we wish to serve that person. If someone says, "I love my country," but when the time comes to defend it, he refuses to be drafted into the military, that is not true love. If someone says, "I love the new book that has been printed," but when she is asked how many times she has read it, she says that she has not read it even once, then people will say, "You have no love for it."

If we love someone, we naturally wish to do something for the happiness of that person. Similarly, *Bhakti* manifests as the desire to serve and glorify God.

Bhakti in All Aspects of Our Life

The amazing thing is that *Bhakti*, or devotion, does not only have to be done in the temple. It can be performed in any place, at any time of the day, and with every action we do. For example, let us say you are a businessman. Without *Bhakti*, you will do business in material consciousness: "Let me earn money so that I can enjoy in the world." If you have love for God, you will still do business, but your attitude will change: "Let me earn a lot of money, so that after taking care of my bodily necessities, I can serve God with it."

Again, if you are a student, you will probably spend a large portion of your day in studying. The material attitude is: "Let me get good results, so that I will become famous and rich." But if one has devotion in the heart, the feelings towards studies will be: "Let me acquire as much knowledge as possible by studying very hard. When I grow up, I will use this knowledge to serve and glorify my Beloved Shree Krishna."

If one is to eat food, the material attitude would be, "Let me eat tasty things and have a good time. It does not matter if I fall sick later, as long as I enjoy myself now." In contrast, if someone possesses *Bhakti*, that person would still be eating food, but with sublime thoughts: "Let me eat good food, so that I may become strong and healthy, and then I will be able to do a lot of service to God."

Bhakti can be Done With All Materials

Bhakti is so encompassing, that it can be done with any material. If you have tasteful fruits and offer them to God with love, He will accept them. But if no fruits are available, you do not have to worry. Take attractive flowers and offer them to Him. If it is peak winter time and flowers are also not available, you still do not need to worry. Get a few leaves and offer them with devotion. If you do not even have leaves, you can simply offer water to God. The Bhagavad Geeta says:

पत्रं पुष्पं फलं तोयं यो मे भक्त्या प्रयच्छति।
तदहं भक्त्युपहृतमश्नामि प्रयतात्मनः।। (भगवद् गीता ९.२६)

patraṁ puṣhpaṁ phalaṁ toyaṁ yo me bhaktyā prayachchhati
tadahaṁ bhaktyupahṛitamaśhnāmi prayatātmanaḥ
(Bhagavad Geeta 9.26)

Shree Krishna says, "If you offer Me with love, a leaf, fruit, flower, or water, I shall accept it." Simply remember that the whole world belongs to God, and use whatever you have to serve Him.

Bhakti was the Basis of the Indian Society

In ancient India, all the arts and sciences developed in the spirit of devotion to God. A majority of the ancient Indian literature was written on the theme of *Bhakti* to the Lord. Hence, we find the Classical Indian dances, such as *Bhārat Nāṭyam, Kathakalī, Kuchipuḍi,* etc. have all got devotion to the Lord as their central theme. Similarly, Indian classical music and all the *rāgas*, or classical melodies, evolved in glorification of God.

There is a very interesting story in this regard. During the Mughal period in India, Akbar became a powerful king of Delhi. Although he was a Muslim, he had great respect for Indian culture. One of the wise men of his court was the great musician, Tansen. It is said that Tansen was so proficient in music, that merely by singing *rāgas*, he could cause rain to fall and lamps to be lighted.

One day, Akbar asked him, "Tansen! You sing so well. Who is the guru from whom you have learnt music?"

Tansen replied, "O King! My Guru is Swami Haridas. He resides in Vrindaban, the holy land of Shree Krishna."

Akbar said, "Please bring him to my court, so that I may be able to see this great person."

"O Emperor! He will not come to your court," said Tansen. "He is a *sanyāsī*. For him, a king and a beggar are both equal. If you wish to meet him, you will have to go to Vrindaban."

Akbar took off his royal attire, and putting on humble garments, he accompanied Tansen to Vrindaban. They went to the hut where Swami Haridas lived. With the desire to hear his Guru singing, Tansen began plucking the strings of the *tānpurā* (stringed Indian musical instrument) and started singing. However, he would deliberately make mistakes.

Finally, with the intention of instructing his student, Swami Haridas said, "That's not the way my son! Let me show you how it is done." Swami Haridas took the *tānpurā* in his hand and began singing. When Akbar heard him, he was delighted.

Later, while returning, Akbar asked Tansen, "Why is it that you cannot sing as well as your Guru can?"

Tansen replied spontaneously, "O King! The reason should

have been obvious to you. I sing for the pleasure of the king of Delhi. My Guru sings for the pleasure of the King of the world. The source of inspiration that Guruji has within himself can never be matched by me."

In this manner, people in ancient India used arts and sciences to glorify God. It was a God-centered society. This was very different from the way Western society developed. The Western world has its roots in the Greek civilization. The epics of the Greeks were Iliad and Odyssey. These are mundane stories of war and romance. In contrast, the epics of the ancient Indian civilization were the Ramayan and Mahabharat. Both these narratives are firmly focused on God, and are full of wisdom and instructions on God-realization. This spirit of *Bhakti* found expression in all aspects of the Indian civilization.

The Glory of India's Ancient Past

With its base in spirituality and God-consciousness, for many centuries, India was considered the pinnacle of human civilization. That greatness slipped out of its hands when it became subjugated to foreign rule. However, the glory of its ancient past has been praised by the greatest minds of the West. This is what some of them have said about India:

"This is India, cradle of the human race, birthplace of human speech, mother of history; the one land that all men desire to see, and having seen once by even a glimpse, would not give that glimpse for all the shows of the rest of the world combined." Mark Twain, American Writer (1835-1910).

"If there is a country on earth that can justly claim the honor of having been the cradle of the human race, or at least the scene of human civilization, the successive developments of

which carried it into all parts of the ancient world, and even beyond, the blessings of knowledge, which is the second life of man, that country is assuredly India." The Encyclopedia Britannica.

"If I were asked under what sky the human mind has most developed some of its choicest gifts, has most deeply pondered on the greatest problems of life, I shall point to India. And if I were to ask myself, from what literature we here in Europe, draw the corrective that is most wanted to make our human life more comprehensive, I shall again point to India." Professor Max Muller, German Orientalist, considered the father of comparative religion (1823 to 1900).

"When India was explored and the wonderful riches of Indian theological literature found, that dispelled once and for all, the dream about Christianity being the sole revelation." Ralph Waldo Emerson, Philosopher (1803-1882).

"I like to think that someone will trace how the deepest thinking of India made its way to Greece, and from there to the philosophy of our times." John Archibald Wheeler, who coined "Black hole" (b-1911).

"By exporting Buddhism to China, India conquered and dominated China culturally for twenty centuries. Hu Shih, former Chinese ambassador to USA (1891-1962).

"The history of India for many centuries had been happier, less fierce, and more dreamlike, than any other history. In these favorable conditions, they built a character, meditative and peaceful, and a nation of philosophers, such as could nowhere have existed except in India." H.G. Wells, Sociologist and Historian (1856-1946).

"The motion of the stars calculated by the Hindus some 4500 years ago, vary not even a single bit from the tables of Casai and Myre, used in the 19th century. The Hindu systems of astronomy are by far the oldest, and that on which the Egyptians, Greeks, and Romans, and even the Jews derived their knowledge." Jean Sylvain Bailly, French Astronomer (1736-1793).

"The Indian way of life provides the vision for the natural, real way of life. We veil ourselves with unnatural masks. On the face of India, are the tender expressions, which carry the marks of the Creator's hands." George Bernard Shaw, Irish Dramatist, Socialist, and Literary critic (1856-1950).

Having discussed the glory of devotion in this chapter, we will now move on to learn how to develop devotion in our hearts.

Chapter 13 Different Manifestations of God

When we desire to do devotion, the first question that will come to mind is: Which form of God should we worship? To understand the answer to this question, we need to know the various aspects of God's personality.

Three Ways in Which God Manifests in the World

God can be realized in varying degrees of closeness. Understand this through an example. Let us say you are standing by the railway tracks. A train is coming from the distance, with its headlight on. It seems to you as if a light is approaching. When the train comes closer, you can see a shimmering form along with the light. Finally, when it comes and stands in front, you realize, "Oh! It's a train. I can see all these people sitting inside their compartments, and peeping out of their windows."

That train seemed like a light from far. As it came closer, it

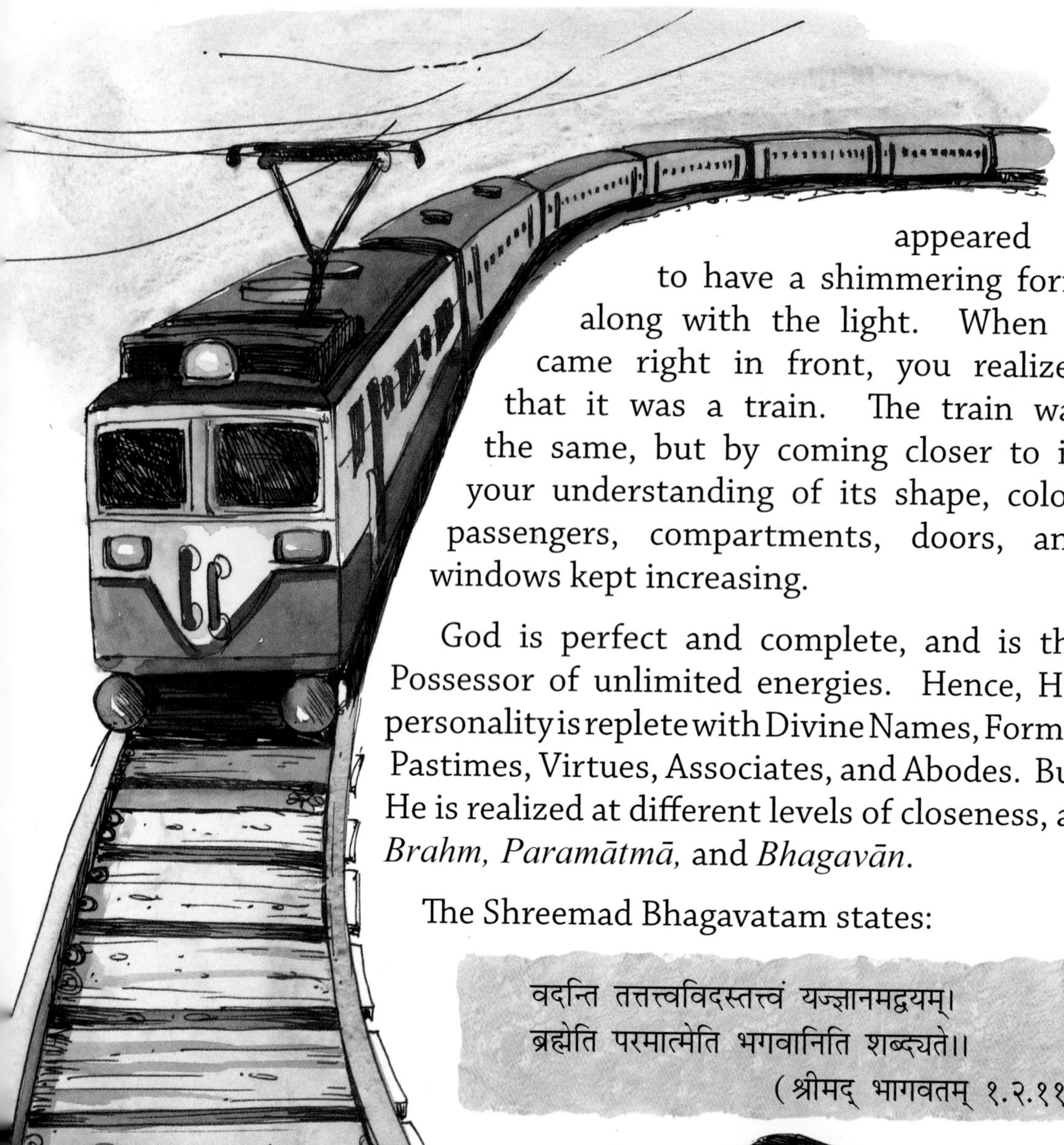

appeared to have a shimmering form along with the light. When it came right in front, you realized that it was a train. The train was the same, but by coming closer to it, your understanding of its shape, color, passengers, compartments, doors, and windows kept increasing.

God is perfect and complete, and is the Possessor of unlimited energies. Hence, His personality is replete with Divine Names, Forms, Pastimes, Virtues, Associates, and Abodes. But He is realized at different levels of closeness, as *Brahm, Paramātmā,* and *Bhagavān*.

The Shreemad Bhagavatam states:

> वदन्ति तत्तत्त्वविदस्तत्त्वं यज्ज्ञानमद्वयम्।
> ब्रह्मेति परमात्मेति भगवानिति शब्द्यते।।
> (श्रीमद् भागवतम् १.२.११)

vadanti tattattvavidastattvaṁ yajgyānamadvayam
brahmeti paramātmeti bhagavāniti śhabdyate
(Shreemad Bhāgavatam 1.2.11)

The learned Sage, Ved Vyas writes: "The Supreme Lord manifests in this world in three ways—*Brahm, Paramātmā,* and *Bhagavān.*" They are not three different Gods, rather they are three manifestations of the one God. However, their qualities are different, just as water, steam, and ice are the same substance, but their physical qualities are different. If some thirsty person asks for water, and you give her a lump of ice, she will say, "What is this? I asked for water."

You may tell her, "Yes, ice is made from Hydrogen Dioxide molecules. It is the same substance as water." That person will reply, "It is the same substance, but its physical properties are different. Ice will not quench my thirst."

Similarly, *Brahm, Paramātmā,* and *Bhagavān* too are different manifestations of the one Supreme Lord, but their qualities are different.

Brahm

This is the aspect of God that is everywhere in creation. The Vedas say:

एको देवः सर्वभूतेषु गूढः सर्वव्यापी... (श्वेताश्वतर उपनिषद् ६.११)

eko devaḥ sarvabhūteṣhu gūḍhaḥ sarvavyāpī...
(Śhvetāśhvatara Upanishad 6.11)

"There is only one God. He is seated in everything and everyone." In this omnipresent aspect, God does not manifest His Forms, Virtues, Pastimes, etc. He is merely existent, full of Eternality, Knowledge, and Bliss.

You may wonder that if God is everywhere, why can't we perceive Him. The reason is that He is Divine, while our senses are all made from the material energy. Hence, our material senses are unable to grasp Him.

Let us say that an ant keeps a lump of salt in its mouth, and goes up a hill of sugar. Another ant walks on the sugar hill along with it. In the evening when they return, the second ant says, "Today I ate so much sugar that I am stuffed with it."

The first ant exclaims, "What are you speaking my dear friend? We were walking on a hill of salt. How did you get to eat sugar?"

The first ant's statement may seem surprising. If they were walking on a hill of sugar, how come the first ant did not experience it? However, if you open its mouth, you will see the lump of salt, which prevented it from tasting the sweetness of the sugar.

Similarly, God is everywhere in creation as the formless *Brahm*. However, our senses are material, and hence, we are unable to perceive Him.

The path of *Gyānyog* gives the realization of God as the all-pervading formless *Brahm*. This is a distant realization of God as a formless Light, just as the train from far appeared to be like light.

Paramātmā

This is the aspect of God that is seated in everyone's hearts. The Bhagavad Geeta states:

ईश्वरः सर्वभूतानां हृद्देशेऽर्जुन तिष्ठति। (भगवद् गीता १८.६१)

īśhvaraḥ sarva bhūtānāṁ hṛiddeśhe 'rjuna tiṣhṭhati
(Bhagavad Geeta 18.61)

Shree Krishna says: "Arjun! God resides in the heart of all living beings." Seated within, He notes all our thoughts and actions, keeps an account of them, and gives the results at the appropriate time. We may forget what we have done, but He does not. If you were asked, "What were you thinking twenty-five hours and fifteen minutes ago?" You would probably say, "I do not remember." However, God remembers what we thought at every moment of our life, since we were born.

And not only for this life! In endless lifetimes, wherever we went, God went along with us, and remained seated in our hearts. In past lives, when we were in a cow's body, God was there with us; when we were in a bird's body, again God was there with us. He is such a Friend of ours, Who never leaves us for even a moment.

That manifestation of God, which is seated in everyone's hearts, is called *Paramātmā*. As the *Paramātmā*, He possesses a Form and Virtues. However, He does not display any Pastimes. The path of *Aṣhṭāṅg Yog* leads to the *Paramātmā* realization of God, residing within our hearts. This is a closer realization, just as the train was seen as a shimmering light form when it came closer.

Bhagavān

This is the aspect of God, when He manifests in His personal form. The Shreemad Bhagavatam states:

कृष्णमेनमवेहि त्वमात्मानमखिलात्मनाम्।
जगद्धिताय सोऽप्यत्र देहीवाभाति मायया।। (श्रीमद् भागवतम् १०.१४.५५)

kṛiṣhṇamenamavehi tvamātmānamakhilātmanām
jagaddhitāya so 'pyatra dehīvābhāti māyayā
(Shreemad Bhagavatam 10.14.55)

"The Supreme Lord Who is the Soul of all souls, manifested in His personal form, as Shree Krishna, for the welfare of the world." That personal form is called *Bhagavān*, in which He manifests all the sweetness of His Names, Forms, Qualities, Abodes, Pastimes, and Associates. These exist in the *Brahm* and *Paramātmā* as well, but they do not manifest, just as a match-stick has fire in it, but it is latent. The fire manifests when it is struck against the igniting strip of the matchbox. Similarly, as *Bhagavān*, all the powers and aspects of God's personality, which are latent in the other forms, get revealed.

The path of *Bhakti*, or devotion, leads to the realization of God in His *Bhagavān* aspect. This is the closest realization of God, just as the details of the train become visible when it comes and stops in front of the observer. Hence, the Bhagavad Geeta states:

भक्त्या मामभिजानाति यावान्यश्चास्मि तत्त्वतः।
ततो मां तत्त्वतो ज्ञात्वा विशते तदनन्तरम्।। (भगवद् गीता १८.५५)

bhaktyā māmabhijānāti yāvānyāśhchāsmi tattvataḥ
tato māṁ tattvato gyātvā viśhate tadanantaram
(Bhagavad Geeta 18.55)

Shree Krishna says: "By devotion alone can I be known in My personal form, as I am, standing before you. With that realization, you can enter into My Being."

The Bliss of the Personal Form of God

Let us say that a woman has married someone, but her husband never allows her to see him, he never allows her to serve him, speak to him, or love him. Wouldn't that wife get exceedingly bored? She would say that I wanted a husband with whom I could sing, dance, play, and love. Similarly, those who worship the formless *Brahm*, cannot see their Lord; they cannot witness His sweet *leelas*; they cannot hear the enchanting sound of His flute, or feel the love of His embrace. They can only experience Him in their minds. But the worshipper of God in the form of *Bhagvān* is able to see the Divine form of His Beloved Lord, participate in His sweet pastimes, and serve Him to his heart's content.

Hence, the highest Bliss of God is attained from His personal form as *Bhagavān*. This is called *Premānand*, or Divine Love Bliss. It is innumerable times sweeter than *Brahmānand*, the Bliss of the formless *Brahm* aspect of God. They are both sweet, but one is sweeter. This is just as jaggery, sugar, and candy are all sweet. However, if you were eating jaggery, and someone put candy in front, you would leave the jaggery and pick up the candy. The jaggery is sweet, but sugar is sweeter, and candy is the sweetest.

Consider another example to understand this point. Let us say that a woman is carrying a baby in her womb. Although she has not seen her baby as yet, she is happy at the thought that soon she will become a mother. After a few months, the baby is born, and starts growing up. Now, the mother holds her one-year old baby in her arms with great love. Ask that mother, "The joy you are experiencing from your baby now, is it the same as the joy you got when the baby was in your womb?"

The mother will say, "What are you saying? That was nine months of pain. This is real bliss. I can see my little daughter, hug her, hear her childish chatter, see her innocent pastimes,

and serve her. That was just a feeling that I have a baby." Similarly, if we worship the formless aspect of God, we will simply get a feeling of God in the mind. If we worship His personal form, we can experience all the sweetness of the Names, Forms, Qualities, Pastimes, Abodes, and Associates.

Besides being more Blissful, worship of the personal form of God is easier as well. If you were asked to watch and think about a light for six hours, you would probably not be able to do so. But if you were asked to see a wonderful drama, with a great story, attractive actors and lots of action, you would enjoy it, and easily sit through it. Similarly, the variety of the attributes of the personal form of God makes devotion to Him much easier.

The Various Personal Forms of God

The Lord eternally exists in His Divine forms in His eternal Abodes, and from time-to-time, He descends on the earth as well, displaying His Divine pastimes here. In the Hindu religion, we are fortunate to have knowledge about the various personal forms of God. The Divine Loving Pastimes of God have also been documented. This makes the path of devotion easy and so much more Blissful. When we engage in devotion with faith in the Divinity of the Forms and Pastimes of God, then our mind become purified with great speed.

Some of the more important Forms of God described in the Hindu scriptures are:

Shree Krishna. He resides eternally in His Divine abode, which is called Golok. About 5000 years ago, Shree Krishna descended on the earth, and displayed sweet loving pastimes that have enchanted billions of people since then. His three-fold bending posture, the peacock crown on His head, His curly hair, and the haunting melody of His flute, have captured the imagination of hundreds of thousands of poet saints. In His Loving pastimes, Shree Krishna revealed how He becomes enslaved by His devotees' love, and even forgets that He is God. Shree Krishna is also the speaker of the Bhagavad Geeta. His pastimes have been described in detail in the Mahabharat and the tenth canto of the Shreemad Bhagavatam.

Shree Ram. His eternal abode is called Saket Lok. He descended on the earth in a previous age called *Tretā Yug*, and displayed the perfect behavior for human beings. He was the ideal son, the ideal brother, ideal friend, and ideal king. Devotees derive great inspiration from the way He discharged His social duties. His charming form and spectacular pastimes make it easy for His devotees to fix their minds on Him. One of His most remembered pastimes is His killing of the demoniac king Ravan, to free Mother Seeta from captivity. These pastimes were described by the ancient poet Valmiki in his great Sanskrit work, the Ramayan, and were later translated in almost every regional language of India.

Lord Vishnu. He oversees the administration of the material worlds. He rests upon the body of Anant Shesh, the Divine snake-form of God. He also resides in everyone's hearts as the *Paramātmā*. Externally, He takes on the four-armed form, with a conch shell, disc, lotus flower, and mace, in His four hands.

His eternal abode in the Divine realm is called Vaikunth, where He resides as Lord Narayan. However, He rarely performs any pastimes. Mother Lakshmi is His eternal consort. In South India, He is commonly worshipped as Vyenkateshwar.

Lord Shiv. He resides in the Divine realm as Sadashiv, and in the material realm as *Bhagavān* Shankar. He displays an exceedingly peaceful nature, and remains in deep meditation in His abode, called Kailash. He has a very merciful mood, and gives shelter to even the lowest kinds of sinners and drunkards. When the time for end of the universe comes, He begins His famous *Tāṇḍav* dance, and winds up all of creation. His eternal consort is Mother Parvati. His Divine pastimes are mentioned in many of the *Purāṇas*, but especially in the Shiv *Purāṇa*.

Radharani. The Divine energy of God manifests in various forms as Radha, Durga, Kali, Lakshmi, Parvati, Amba, Rukmini, etc. They are all called the Divine Mother of the Universe. The motherly aspect of God is full of beauty, gentleness, kindness, and tenderness. The sweetest form of the Divine Mother is Radha. She is the Divine energy of Shree Krishna and it is by Her power that He manifests His amazing Pastimes, Divine Abode, and Divine Bliss. Radharani possesses the highest level of selfless Divine Love, and so She occupies the topmost place in Shree Krishna's *leelas*. By Her Grace, the souls receive pure love for Shree Krishna, and attain His loving service.

Mother Durga. She is in charge of the functioning of the material energy. Hence, She is worshipped as the Divine Mother of the world and of all the souls residing in the material realm. The worship of God in the form of Mother is unique to Hinduism. Just as a child believes its mother to be all-powerful and capable of doing anything for the child, a devotee believes the Divine Mother to be All-merciful, All-powerful, and eternally

protecting him with Her invisible arms.

Ganesh. He is the remover of obstacles, and hence He is traditionally worshipped or remembered in the beginning of auspicious works as Vighneshwar (one who removes impediments). He is the giver of knowledge, so He is also called Vinayak (knowledgeable). In His Divine pastimes, Ganesh is the older son of Lord Shiv and Mother Parvati. He has four hands, an elephant's head, and a big belly.

Hanuman. He is a great devotee of Lord Ram, endowed with heroic qualities. His devotion to His Lord is immense, and in His service, He does not hesitate to undertake the most herculean tasks. He carries a *gadā*, or mace, which is a sign of His bravery and heroism. He leads a life of renunciation and austerity, presenting an ideal for the inspiration of everyone who hears about His pastimes.

We shall now discuss how to engage in devotion to God, to have His closest realization and experience the Bliss of Divine Love. 卐

Chapter 14 Divine Love–The Greatest Treasure

The Powers of God

All of us have many powers—the power to see, hear, think, and so on. If a particular power of someone reduces, that person becomes handicapped. For example, if someone says, "I am blind," it means that the person's power to see has finished. We need multiple powers to accomplish any task.

We souls possess powers that are limited, both in number and in extent. God is called *Sarva-śhaktimān*, which means He is All-powerful. He possesses innumerable powers, and each is unlimited in extent. By virtue of these powers, He is full of Knowledge, full of Bliss, the Creator of the world, and the accomplisher of humanely impossible tasks. He creates this world out of His material power, called Maya. He also has a superior spiritual power, which is called *Yogamāyā*. You can imagine that if God's material power is so amazing that it creates such an incredible world, how amazing will His spiritual power be? All the Divine *leelas* of Shree Krishna and Shree Ram that we read about, were accomplished by that spiritual power, *Yogamāyā*.

The Power of Divine Love

Yogamāyā has many branches. The highest of these is the power of Divine Love. This is God's most extraordinary power. It is so special that if someone possesses Divine Love, God feels obliged to become a servant of that devotee. The Shreemad Bhagavatam states:

अहं भक्तपराधीनो ह्यस्वतन्त्र इव द्विज।
साधुभिर्ग्रस्तहृदयो भक्तैर्भक्तजनप्रियः।। (श्रीमद् भागवतम् ९.४.६३)

ahaṁ bhaktaparādhīno hyasvatantra iva dvija
sādhubhirgrastahṛidayo bhaktairbhaktajanapriyaḥ
(Shreemad Bhagavatam 9.4.63)

Shree Krishna states: "I am supremely independent, but Divine Love is such a power that it binds Me. My devotees who possess it have won My heart, and are very dear to Me."

Whenever God descends in this world, He reveals such loving pastimes, where He shows how He is captured by the love of His devotees. There are innumerable verses to this extent:

व्यापक ब्रह्म निरँजन निर्गुण विगत विनोद।
सो अज प्रेम भगति बस कौसल्या कें गोद।। (रामायण)

vyāpaka brahma nirañjana nirguṇa vigata vinoda
so aja prema bhagati basa kausalyā keñ goda (Ramayan)

"We all know that God is all-pervading in this world. We also

know about His formless aspect. However, look at the power of Kaushalya's *Bhakti*, under whose spell, the very same Supreme Lord has become a small baby and is lying in her lap."

श्रुतिमपरे स्मृतिमितरे भारतमन्ये भजन्तु भवभीताः।
अहमिह नन्दं वन्दे यस्या लिन्दे परं ब्रह्म।। (पद्यावली)

śhrutimapare smṛitimitare bhāratamanye bhajantu bhavabhītāḥ
ahamiha nandaṁ vande yasyā linde paraṁ brahma (Padyāvalī)

"That God, Who is unknowable even through the scriptures, has become the son of Nand Baba. I offer my obeisance to that great soul—Nand Baba—in whose house the Supreme Lord is playing like a child."

जो नहीं जात बुलायेहु, शुक सनकादिक ध्यान।
बिनुहिँ बुलाये जात सोइ, घर घर ब्रजवनितान।।
(जगद्गुरु श्री कृपालुजी महाराज)

jo nahīñ jāta bulāyehu, śhuka sanakādika dhyāna
binuhiñ bulāye jāta soi, ghara ghara vrajavanitāna
(Jagadguru Shree Kripaluji Maharaj)

"Look at the glory of Divine Love. That Supreme Lord, Who hesitates to reveal Himself in the *samādhi* of great personalities, like Shukadev and Sanat Kumar, goes uninvited to the house of the *gopīs* of Braj." The wonderfully amazing *leelas*, or pastimes, revealed in the above verses show that God is Himself under the power of Divine Love. A very sweet pastime of the Lord that illustrates this point is described below.

The Lord Gets Tied by a Rope

The Supreme Lord descended in the world as Shree Krishna, and performed loving pastimes with His devotees. Although He is the Lord of all the worlds, He became a little child, playing with His cowherd friends and stealing butter from the *gopīs*.

Once when He was small, Mother Yashoda was churning butter in the kitchen. Although she was pulling the rope with her hands, her mind was absorbed in loving thoughts of Krishna. She was thinking, "Let me churn very soft and sweet butter, so that I may feed Krishna with it and give Him much happiness."

Shree Krishna reached the scene. Finding His mother busy

churning butter, He desired her affectionate attention. So He climbed into her lap, caught her face with His tiny hands, and tried to make her look in His direction. Observing her dear Krishna's naughtiness gave great pleasure to Mother Yashoda. She began feeding Him milk with immense love, while fondling Him affectionately. Krishna was enjoying His mother's affection.

In the meantime, the milk in the pot, on the fire, started boiling and overflowing. Seeing this, Mother Yashoda hurriedly put Krishna aside and ran to take the milk off the fire. Krishna was annoyed that His mother had left Him to tend to the milk, as if it were more important than Him. To let Mother Yashoda know that He was angry, He took the churning rod and smashed the pot of butter. He also broke some more pots nearby. Then He carried a small pot of butter out of the house. He ate some butter Himself and began feeding the rest to the monkeys.

Having taken care of the milk, Mother Yashoda returned to the butter. She was shocked to see all the pots smashed. She decided to teach her little son a lesson, and taking a rod in her hand, she came out of the house. Finding His mother so angry, Krishna ran to save Himself from a beating. His four steps were equal to one of Yashoda's, as she chased Him. However, He was still quicker than His mother, and she became tired.

The Lord is faster than the fastest, so who can catch Him? However, seeing Yashoda's exhaustion, Krishna felt pity on her, and pretended to get tired Himself. He slowed down, allowing Mother Yashoda to catch hold of Him. God is the Father of all souls, but because of Yashoda's love, He had subjected Himself to the role of her child.

The mother has the right to punish her child for his betterment,

and so Yashoda took a rope to bind Krishna to the grinding wheel. However, the rope turned out to be two fingers short! So Yashoda tied a second rope to the first one and again tried to bind Krishna. But again the rope was two fingers short! No matter how many ropes Yashoda kept adding, the rope was still not long enough to tie Krishna. God is bigger than the whole universe, which resides inside Him. Unless He Himself allows it, who can ever tie Him?

Mother Yashoda was bewildered! Finally, Krishna again felt pity on her and allowed Himself to be tied. Thus the scriptures state:

यशोदया समाकपि देवता नास्ति भूतले।
उलूखले यया बद्धो मुक्तिदो मुक्तिमिच्छति।।

yaśhodayā samākapi devatā nāsti bhūtale
ulūkhale yayā baddho muktido muktimichchhati

"Can any *devatā* be considered as fortunate as Mother Yashoda? That Lord, who releases the souls from the bonds of Maya, has been tied by her with a rope, and is begging her for His release." This amazing pastime reveals the glory of Divine love, and shows how the devotee can bind the Supreme Lord with his or her love.

Krishna's Loving Pastimes Confounded Even Brahma

When Shree Krishna was four years old, the Sage Narad went to his father, the celestial god Brahma, and said, "Father, do you know the Supreme Lord has descended in our universe. He is displaying His Divine pastimes in the land of Braj, in India."

Brahma ji desired to see the Lord, and he went with Narad to

Braj. At that time, Shree Krishna was sitting and eating food with His cowherd friends, while their cows were grazing in the forest. Astonishingly, Shree Krishna was eating the remnants from the plates of His friends. Brahma ji was shocked, "How can this be God? He is eating the food remnants of these little village boys!"

Narad said, "Father, if you do not wish to believe me, I am going." Saying this, Narad Muni went away.

Brahma ji began thinking, "Narad was so serious about it; can this child really be God? But this kind of behavior is not becoming of God. He seems to be an ordinary boy to me." Finally, Brahma ji decided to do a test. By His power, he made all the cowherd boys and the cows disappear. He transferred them to a cave located in the *Sumeru* Mountain of heaven. He thought that if this child was God, He would come to know. But if he was not God, he would start crying, "Where have my friends and cows gone?"

For the all-knowing Lord Krishna, it was no problem to know what had happened. He decided to teach Brahma ji a lesson. So He made His form like Brahma and went to Brahma-lok, the abode of Brahma. There He told the guard, "A false Brahma will come shortly. Do not let him into the palace." The guard agreed to do as he had been told.

Then Shree Krishna took on all the forms of His cows and cowherd friends Himself. In each form, He kept doing all their routine works. So neither the mothers of the children, nor anyone else in Braj came to know that the real children and cows had been taken to *Sumeru* Mountain.

After hiding the children, Brahma ji returned to his abode. However, he was stopped by the guard who accused him of

being a false Brahma. Brahma wondered what the matter was, and suspected that it may have to do with the boy in Braj. He went back quickly to Braj on the earth planet. However, by earthly calculations, one full year had passed. What Brahma ji saw, amazed him completely. Just as before, Shree Krishna was sitting with His cowherd friends, eating their remnants, while the cows grazed nearby.

Brahma ji was shocked. He went running back to Sumeru Mountain. There he found the cowherd boys and cows, just as he had placed them. Then Brahma ji realized, "Oh my God! That boy is the Supreme Lord Himself. How impudent of me to think of testing Him!" He returned to Braj again to apologize.

This time, Shree Krishna displayed His Divine four-armed Shree Vishnu form in all the children and cows present. Brahma ji fell at Shree Krishna's feet, and profusely praised the good fortune of the boys, whose friend the Lord had Himself become. Brahma ji prayed:

तदस्तु मे नाथ स भूरिभागो भवेऽत्र वान्यत्र तु वा तिरश्चाम्।
येनाहमेकोऽपि भवज्जनानां भूत्वा निषेवे तव पादपल्लवम्।।
(श्रीमद् भागवतम् १०.१४.३०)

tadastu me nātha sa bhūribhāgo
bhave' tra vānyatra tu vā tiraśhchām
yenāhameko 'pi bhavajjanānāṁ
bhūtvā niṣheve tava pādapallavam (Shreemad Bhagavatam)

"My Lord! In my next life, do not give me the seat of Brahma. Make me a blade of grass in this land of Braj. Then I will be able to get the dust of the lotus feet of these cowherd friends of Yours, and I too will receive the Divine Love that they possess."

There are hundreds of such pastimes, which reveal how God forgets His Almightiness before His devotees. He becomes their Friend, Child, and even Beloved. These *leelas* are revealed in the Vedic scriptures, which is one of the many features that make Hinduism so special.

The Greatest Treasure We Can Possess

Divine Love is such a power that if someone possesses it, God happily serves that devotee. That is why in the Mahabharat war, Shree Krishna drove the chariot, while Arjun merrily sat on it. Shree Krishna is the Supreme Master of the universe, while Arjun was a mere soul. However, Arjun was such a soul, who possessed Divine Love, and hence Shree Krishna took the position of serving him.

This is the glory of Divine Love, in front of which all worldly treasures become tiny. Also, while other treasures will remain behind when we leave this world, the treasure of Divine Love will go with us after death. Thus, it is the highest treasure that we can possess. Saint Kabir said:

कबीरा सब जग निर्धना धन्वंता नहिं कोय।
धन्वंता सोइ जानिए जाहि प्रेम धन होय।।

kabīrā saba jaga nirdhanā dhanvañtā nahiñ koya
dhanvañta soi jāniye jāhi prema dhana hoya

"Nobody in this world is really wealthy, except that person, who possesses the wealth of Divine Love."

However, since it is such an invaluable thing, God does not give Divine Love easily. We must now try to find out how we can receive this priceless treasure. 卐

Chapter 15 Developing Our Relationship with God

The Need to Purify the Mind

God does not easily bestow Divine Love, since it is His highest power, and the ultimate thing one can possess. He waits till the devotee becomes deserving of it. So if we want Divine Love, we will have to qualify ourselves for it. This qualification is not an external certificate or degree; it is the preparation of the heart and mind. We will have to purify our mind completely, to have the good fortune of receiving Divine Love.

Only in a pure mind, can such an amazing power reside. This is just as if you wish to invite some important person to your house; you will first clean and tidy the house. Instead, if you have a dead dog lying on your drawing room carpet, and your guest comes, she will depart in a hurry, saying, "What an awful place! The stink is unbearable." Similarly, Divine Love is like a Queen. If we wish it to reside in our mind, we will have to make the mind pure like a temple of God.

Preparatory Devotion

How will the mind be cleansed? This will happen through "preparatory devotion". Such devotion will prepare the vessel of the mind, in which God will then bestow His Divine Love. Hence, *Bhakti* is of two kinds:

1. *Sādhan Bhakti*, or Preparatory devotion. *Sādhan Bhakti* is what we will have to do to cleanse the mind from anger, greed, lust, envy, pride, and illusion.

2. *Siddha Bhakti*, or Divine Love. *Siddha Bhakti* is a Divine power that we will receive by God's Grace.

The purification of the mind is a natural consequence of doing *Sādhan Bhakti*. God is all-pure, beyond the three modes of material nature. When we attach our mind to Him, it starts rising above the three modes. First, *tamo guṇa*, the mode of ignorance, is destroyed. Then, *rajo guṇa*, the mode of passion is finished, and the mind becomes *sāttvic*, or established in the mode of goodness. Finally, by the Grace of God, the *sattva guṇa* is also destroyed, and the mind is made Divine. At this stage, *Sādhan Bhakti* is complete, and the vessel is ready for receiving *Siddha Bhakti*. So to get Divine Love, we must first learn how to do preparatory devotion.

Our Eternal Relationship with God

The first point in *Sādhan Bhakti* is to develop our relationship with God. We souls are His eternal parts, and hence we have an everlasting relationship with Him. The worldly relatives keep changing from lifetime-to-lifetime. In your previous life, you had a different set of father, mother, sister, brother, and friends. In the life before that, you had another set of relatives. However, God is our eternal Father, Mother, Friend, and Relative. He is such a Friend, Who does not leave us for even a moment. In endless lifetimes, wherever we went, God went with us. When we went into a cat's body, God accompanied us. When we went into a cow's body, God went with us there as well.

God is also such a Friend, who is totally selfless. Since He is perfect and complete in Himself, He does not need anything from us. So He always acts for our welfare and benefit. There is a beautiful story in this regard.

Once, during the course of his long journey, a traveler reached a village after midnight. He was hungry and tired. He saw a light in one house, and so he knocked on the door. When the owner came out, the traveler folded his hands, and pleaded, "Sir, I have come from far, and I am very hungry. Can I get something to eat at your home?"

The house-owner replied, "In our village there is a very generous person. Nobody goes disappointed from his door. Go to his house, and he will take good care of you." He guided the traveler to the generous person's house.

The traveler reached there, and knocked on the door. The benevolent person was sleeping soundly when he heard the knock. He opened the door, while rubbing his eyes. The traveler asked, "Sir! I have heard from others that you are a very kind man, and no one who comes for charity to your door, goes away disappointed. I have journeyed from far, and am very hungry. Can I please have something to eat?"

The kind person said, "My dear fellow! You have come at an unearthly hour. Everyone in my home is sleeping. However, please do come in and wait a while. Let me see what I can arrange." He brought the traveler into his drawing room.

An hour-and-a-half later, he brought a plate of food, and put it on the table before the guest. "This has been arranged by the Grace of God," he said. "Please accept this humble offering, and bestow your blessings upon me."

The traveler was an atheist. "Why have you brought God into the picture," he blurted. "It has been cooked by you. God has nothing to do with it."

The generous person was taken aback on hearing this. "Do you not believe in God?" he asked.

"Of course not!" replied the traveler. "He is a figment of our imagination. We do the work, and give God the credit for it."

The kind person was infuriated. He pulled the plate away, and shoved the traveler out of his house, saying, "Let me see how you can get food without the Grace of God." He went back to bed, and soon fell asleep.

In his dream, God appeared vividly. The benevolent person offered obeisance to God in the dream. God asked him, "You kicked that traveler out of your house?"

"My Lord, he was abusing You. How could I stand it?"

"How old did he appear to you?" God asked.

"He seemed to be about fifty-five years old."

"Do you know that he has been abusing Me for the last forty years?" God said. "And yet, I ensure that he gets his meals three times a day. You could not tolerate his abuses even once!"

The generous man fell at God's feet, "My Lord, who can be as merciful as You! You provide the air, earth, water, and food, even to those who deny Your existence."

The above story illustrates what a kind and merciful Friend God is. He takes care even of those souls who abuse Him.

God's Grace Comes in Many Ways

If God is so merciful, and is our eternal Friend, then why do we suffer in the world? This question arises in the minds of many people. The answer is that God does not violate the law of karma. God merely gives us the results of our own karmas.

करम प्रधान विश्व करि राखा।
जो जस करइ सो तस फलु चाखा।। (रामायण)

karama pradhāna viśhva kari rākhā
jo jasa karai so tasa phalu chākhā (Ramayan)

"Everyone gets the good or bad results of their own activities. The law of karma prevails in the world." However, the karmas are noted by God, and the results,both—sweet and bitter—are given by Him. So we should realize the Grace of God in both—sweet and bitter experiences. Even the worldly mother showers her love on the child in various ways. Sometimes she affectionately hugs her child, and sometimes she says, "Go, stand by the wall. I will not speak to you." At times she cooks delicious foodstuffs for the child, and at times she says, "Your stomach is upset. You will not get anything." All these behaviors are forms of the mother's tender affection for her child.

Similarly, the Divine Mother, the Supreme Lord, also bestows His Grace in different ways. If He gives us suffering according to our karmas, that is also for our benefit. It is a signal that we did wrong, and we should improve ourselves. All suffering should be viewed with this positive attitude.

There is the story of a boy, who noticed a beautiful cocoon on a tree. He would watch it every day in order to have the first glimpse of the butterfly that would emerge. Finally, one day he saw a tiny hole in the cocoon that grew as the hours passed. He sat watching the butterfly break her way out of the cocoon. However, suddenly he noticed that the butterfly seemed to stop making progress. The hole did not get larger and the butterfly appeared to be stuck. The cocoon was bouncing up and down as the butterfly tried unsuccessfully to squeeze herself out.

The boy took a small pair of scissors and cut the cocoon, allowing the butterfly to emerge easily. However, instead of soaring gracefully into the sky, the butterfly dropped to the

ground. The boy noticed that the butterfly's stomach was swollen but her wings were small and shriveled. He assumed that after some time, the stomach would shrink and the wings would inflate. However, this was never to be.

The boy did not know that it was the very act of forcing herself out of the cocoon that would have pushed the fluid from the butterfly's stomach into her wings. Without that external pressure, the stomach would always remain swollen and the wings would always be shriveled.

In life too, we often avoid challenges, looking for the easy way out. We look for people who will "cut our cocoons" so that we never have to work and push our way through difficulties.

However, little do we realize that it is going through those hard times that prepare us for the road ahead. The obstacles in our path are God's way of making us able to fly. With every bit of pushing and struggling, our wings become fuller and fuller. What we call bad destiny is actually an opportunity for growth.

Coming Closer to God

Although God is our selfless Friend, the problem is that we have forgotten our relationship with Him since innumerable lifetimes. So we will need to put some effort to remember it. Suppose you had a friend who had been very close to you in Grade One. However, she had shifted to another city with her parents. You meet her after a gap of seven years. You thumped her on the back, and asked, "Anita! What a pleasure to meet you after so long?"

Your friend did not recognize you. She looked at you in puzzlement. "Who are you?" she asked.

"You did not recognize me? We used to study together in Grade One."

"O yes, I have a faint recollection of us being together."

"Sometimes we would do biking together!"

"Yes...yes, I am remembering more now."

"We lived in the same neighborhood. And our parents would drive us together to school."

"O yes, now I remember! You are Sheila."

We see how Anita was a friend of Sheila, but she had forgotten, and so she required some effort to remember. Similarly, God is our eternal Relative, but we have forgotten Him. So it will require some effort on our part to recollect that relationship. That is what *Sādhan Bhakti* will help us to do.

Another name for *Sādhan Bhakti* is *upāsanā*. The word *upāsanā* means to come close to God. How can we do that? By thinking, "He is mine." We can think, "Shree Krishna is my Father. Radharani is my Mother." Or if wish, we can think, "Shree Krishna is my Friend." Just as the cowherd boys of Braj looked upon Shree Krishna as their friend. We then have the privilege to play with Him, and confide in Him.

We can even think that Shree Krishna is our Beloved. This is how the *gopīs* of Vrindaban worshipped Shree Krishna. A great example of this *bhāv* (sentiment of devotion) was Meera Bai. She looked upon the Lord as her Beloved, and in this way, felt the greatest proximity with Him. We too can increase our love for Shree Krishna, by establishing sweet loving relationships with Him.

Devotion may sometimes seem very similar to worldly love, but actually it is totally the opposite. The distinction is that love in the world is selfish, while true Love for God is selfless. We shall learn about selfless love in the next chapter.卐

Chapter 16 Selfless Love

Do Not Ask God for Worldly Things

If we approach God with worldly desires, our mind remains stuck in the world. Then no matter how much devotion we do, the mind does not become pure. It is like packing dirty water in a bottle, and dipping the bottle in the holy *Ganga*. No matter how long the bottle remains in the *Ganga*, the water within stays dirty, since it does not even come in contact with the water of the *Ganga*.

A humorous story illustrates this point nicely. There were two neighbors, Ramesh and Dinesh. As sometimes happens between neighbors, they developed great envy for each other. When one bought a new car, the other did the same. One built a fence around his yard, and the other followed suit. One repainted the exterior of his house, and shortly afterwards, the other also did it.

After a few years of living as neighbors, their animosity increased to such an extent that they could not tolerate seeing each other. Finally, Ramesh thought of an idea to get ahead of Dinesh. He decided that he would please Lord Shiv and ask Him for a boon. The next day, early in the morning, at 5 AM, he went to the temple of Lord Shiv. He offered his obeisance to the *Shiv Liṅg*, and sat down under a tree in the courtyard of the temple. He began chanting, "*Oṁ Namaḥ Shivaya*!" with the resolve that he would not stop until Lord Shiv appeared before him and asked him what he wanted.

However, sometimes evil minds think alike. On the previous night, Dinesh too had gotten the same idea, that he would get ahead of Ramesh by asking Lord Shiv for a boon. So at 5.15 AM, he reached the same temple. He offered his obeisance to the *Shiv Liṅg*, and sat down in the courtyard under another tree.

Sounds of "*Oṁ Namaḥ Shivaya*" came to his ears. He looked in that direction, and was shocked to see his neighbor Ramesh sitting under the other tree. He immediately guessed Ramesh's intention, and resolved, "Let's see who will get a boon from Lord Shiv first." He too began chanting the name of Shiv.

At around 7 AM, devotees began coming to the temple. They found Ramesh and Dinesh sitting and chanting the Names of God, apparently in great devotion. They thought, "These two have such concentration of mind. They must be great devotees."

At noon time, Mother Parvati said to God Shiv, "Ramesh and Dinesh are taking Your name with such intensity. Why don't You go and give them Your *darśhan*?"

Shiv ji replied, "Parvati, they will not benefit from it. But if You say so, I will go to them."

He first appeared before Ramesh, and said, "My son, I have come. Open your eyes." Ramesh opened his eyes, and saw Lord Shiv before him. Shiv ji asked, "What do you want? Ask and I will give it to you."

Ramesh said, "My Lord! I will definitely ask. However before I do, I have a question. Have You given *darśhan* to Dinesh as yet?"

"I have not," said God Shiv. "But after this, I intend to go to him."

Ramesh was now in a fix. If he asked for a Mercedes, Dinesh would ask for two Mercedes; if he asked for a million dollars, Dinesh would ask for two million dollars. Finally, he had an idea. He said, "O Lord! Whatever you give to Dinesh, give me twice of that."

Shiv ji then went before Dinesh and said, "My son, I have come; open your eyes. What do you want from me?"

Dinesh offered his obeisance to God Shiv. He too asked, "O Lord, before I request for a boon, please tell me whether You have given *darśhan* to Ramesh?"

"That I have," replied Shiv ji.

"What did he ask?"

"He said that whatever you get, he should get double."

Dinesh was in the fix now. Having performed such severe austerities, he would still remain behind Ramesh. Finally, an idea came to him for getting ahead. He said, "Please make blind in one eye."

Lord Shiv granted the boon; He made Dinesh blind in one eye, and Ramesh became totally blind. The people, who had been thinking that these two were great devotees, realized that they were not devotees at all. Although they had been taking the name of God, their minds were steeped in worldly desires.

True devotion is that where the mind gets attached to God. If physically we worship God, but our mind is attached to the world, it will be devotion to the world and not to God. Such devotion will not cleanse the mind from the afflictions of Maya. Hence, if we want to purify our mind, we must strictly follow the rule of not asking God for worldly things. It is such devotion that will cleanse the mind.

The Golden Rule

Some people look upon God as an order supplier. They think they will ask Him for material things, and He will surely give them whatever they ask. However, God is not a fulfiller of our demands. As was mentioned earlier, He has rules, according to which He governs the world. The golden rule is that we get what we deserve.

A Christian priest once said, "I heard the prayers of hundreds of people. Each of them was praying, 'O God! Why is two plus two equal to four? Why is it not equal to ten?" What he meant was that someone did a bad action and got a bad result. Now that person prayed, "Although by my actions I deserve misery, please give me great fortune." This is like praying for two plus two to be equal to ten and not four. But we must remember that God will not give us what we desire; He will give us what we deserve.

Selfish Love Keeps Fluctuating

In the world, we often experience that our love for others

keeps varying. The same father, mother, sister, brother, friend, teacher, sometimes appear very nice, sometimes they appear normal, and sometimes we start hating them. We find that our love for them does not remain steady.

The reason for this is that we do not love them selflessly. We want something from them. When our self-interest is fulfilled, we think that they are very nice. When our self-interest is not fulfilled, we feel that they are just normal. And when our self-interest gets harmed, we dislike them. If we loved them selflessly, then no matter how they behaved with us, our love for them would not reduce.

Similarly, if we love God selfishly, then our devotion will keep fluctuating. The advantage of selfless love will be that our devotion will steadily keep increasing.

Seek God and All Else Will Be Added

Shree Krishna is the Supreme Master of unlimited universes. He possesses unimaginable treasures that He is anxious to bestow upon the soul. Asking Him for material things, is like meeting Kuber, the celestial god of wealth, and asking him for one dollar. People would laugh if someone were to do that. Similarly, one who asks Shree Krishna for material things, has no knowledge of the treasures in the Divine realm.

A king once went to a foreign country. From there, he wrote to his queens, asking them what they would like him to bring for them. All the queens responded with expensive requests. The youngest queen simply wrote the numeral "1" on her letter to the king. When the king returned, he had brought the things that were requested by the other queens. He asked his servants to carry them to their respective rooms. But for the youngest

1

queen, he went to her palace himself, and asked, "What was the meaning of the "1" that you wrote? What did you want?"

The intelligent queen replied, "The "1" meant that I wanted you only, nothing else; and I have gotten you. Thank you so much!"

In the same way, if we make the world as our goal, we will not attain God. But if we make God as our goal, we will automatically get all of God's Knowledge, Love, and Bliss. However, we must remember to love God, and not do business with Him.

Difference between Business and Love

Business is an activity that involves give and take. We give something to the other party, and in return, we seek something for ourselves. If what we get is more than what we have given, the business is considered profitable. But if it is less, then the business is considered unprofitable. Someone engaged in business is always concerned about what he or she will get in return.

When we engage in devotion to God, we often do the same mistake. We go to His temple, but ask God for material things. This is like doing business with Him. This is like a trader, who says, "O God! Give me five million dollars profit, and I will donate fifty thousand to the temple." The trader is making the blunder of trying to engage God in a deal.

If we love someone so that we will get something in return, it no longer remains love; it becomes a business deal. Selfless love is the opposite of business. In such love, we desire only to give...give... give, without considering what we will get.

The Importance of Giving

Selfless love is free from all self-seeking. However, to desire happiness is the nature of the soul. If selfless devotees do not desire their own happiness, then what do they seek? The answer to this question is that they desire the pleasure of God. They love Shree Krishna for the sake of His happiness. And to make Him happy, they wish to serve Him with whatever they have.

What can we give to God? We have three possessions, with which we can serve Him:

1. **Mind:** Bring such thoughts to the mind that will make Shree Krishna happy.

2. **Body:** Engage the body in service activities for the pleasure of God.

3. **Wealth:** Donate a portion of the income to causes that are pleasing to God.

Amongst these, serving with the mind is the most important, then comes the body, and finally, wealth. But to reach to the point where the mind remains engaged in loving thoughts, we must begin from below. We must learn to serve God with our wealth. Then we will develop the desire to engage the body in service as well. And when the body is engaged, the mind will naturally begin meditating on giving happiness to God.

That is why the scriptures instruct:

न्यायोपार्जित वित्तस्य दशमांशेन धीमतः।
कर्तव्यो विनियोगश्च ईश्वरप्रित्यर्थमेव च।। (स्कन्ध पुराण)

nyāyopārjita vittasya daśhamānśhena dhīmataḥ
kartavyo viniyogaśhcha īśhvaraprityarthameva cha
(Skandha Purāṇa)

"Whatever you have earned by genuine means, take out one-tenth from it, and donate it in charity in the service of God. That is your duty." This practice of donating one-tenths of one's income has many benefits. It prevents one from misusing additional wealth. It develops the service attitude towards God. It expands the heart of the devotee. It teaches the devotee to practice selfless love. This is the rule in Hinduism, which is also being practiced by other religions.

We will next discuss the need for meditation and its techniques, increasing our love for God. 卐

Chapter 17 How to Practice Devotion Daily

The Need for Regular Practice

To progress in devotion, we must practice it daily. Nobody can hope to become physically strong, by drinking five pounds of *ghee*, clarified butter, on a just single day. It is by eating and drinking healthy food on a daily basis that we become strong. Similarly, spiritual progress does not come merely by doing devotion only on special occasions. We must set up a daily practice of *Bhakti*. This regular practice will gradually and systematically increase the attachment of our mind towards God. It will increase our spiritual strength, just as daily exercises increase physical strength, and regular studies increases intellectual strength. There is a saying:

क्षणसः क्षणसो विद्या कणसः कणसो धनम्।

kṣhaṇasaḥ kṣhaṇaso vidyā kaṇasaḥ kaṇaso dhanam

"By carefully saving single dollars at a time, a person becomes a millionaire. By using each possible moment to study, one becomes a scholar." Similarly, by daily engaging in the practice of devotion, one attains Divine Love.

Where to do Devotion

We live in the material world, and are constantly bombarded by its influences. Television channels, magazines, newspapers, internet, video games, etc., all pull our mind towards the world. In such an environment, it becomes difficult to think of God. So our daily devotion must be done in a place where the world cannot disturb us.

If you have a worship room in your house, that is the best. Else, you can set aside a small corner of your house, or your own bedroom for your devotional practice. The place should be big enough for the altar and for the family members to sit. You must create a sacred atmosphere in that place, so that when you sit there, the mind gets naturally transported to the Divine realm.

If you have wooden temple in your home, that is perfect. Else you can make the altar on a suitable table, covered with a nice piece of cloth. The altar should have images of Radha Krishna and your Guru. You can also have small flower-vases around the altar to beautify it, and decorate it tastefully. You must think that God is actually present in that image, and hence decorate your worship room for His pleasure.

You can also keep incense sticks and a holder for placing them. Lighting incense sticks creates an aroma that many people find sacred. For the *ārati*, you will need an *ārati* plate, lamp, and wicks. Another plate can be kept for food offerings.

The Principle behind Deity Worship

Our mind is naturally attracted to forms and shapes. If you were asked to love a white light, you would find it almost impossible, since the mind would feel no attraction towards it. That is why, even religious traditions that worship God as a light, use sacred symbols to aid remembrance of Him, such as the Holy Cross, the Moon and Star, etc.

In the Vedic tradition, we are fortunate to have more powerful and blissful ways of remembering the Lord. Based on the descriptions of the Forms of God in the Vedas and *Purāṇas*, deities are made from stone, wood, metal, etc. These deities are

installed in temples, with great faith and devotion. The Lord is then requested to manifest in that Deity, for receiving the devotion and offerings made by the devotees. God is present everywhere, so why would He not be present in His Deity. He truly resides in the Deity and reciprocates the love of His devotees. When His image is in front of us, it becomes easier to think of Him and love Him. That is the principle behind the Deity worship in Hindu temples around the world.

However, Deity worship has many rules that must be adhered to. It is suitable for the temple, but for your own home, it requires a deep commitment to rules and regulations. If you have such a commitment, you can go ahead and install deities in your house, or else there is a simpler option. Place pictures of your Beloved Radha Krishna and Gurudev on your altar. Now without having to bother about cumbersome rules, you will be able to look at Their Divine Forms and increase your love and devotion. These are your picture deities. In the next chapter, you will be learning how to take the help of pictures to meditate on God.

The Importance of *Kīrtan*

You would like to bring Divine thoughts to your mind. *Kīrtan* is the greatest way of doing that. It involves three activities: (1) Chanting the Names, and descriptions of the Forms, Virtues, Pastimes, and Prayers to the Lord in melodious tunes. (2) Hearing the chanting with your ears. (3) Thinking deeply about what you are chanting, and feeling the presence of God in His Holy Name. *Kīrtan* is the combination of all three of these activities, and hence it is also called *Tridhā Bhakti*, or three-fold devotion.

This *Kīrtan* is called the *Yug Dharma*, or the most powerful

spiritual practice of this age. The chanting and hearing are important aids to remembering God. *Kīrtan* is also so simple, that anyone can do it.

The Scriptures state:

कलेर्दोषनिधे राजन्नस्ति ह्येको महान् गुणः।
कीर्तनाद् एव कृष्णस्य मुक्तसङ्गः परं व्रजेत्।। (श्रीमद् भागवतम् १२.३.५१)

kalerdoṣhanidhe rājannasti hyeko mahān guṇaḥ
kīrtanād eva kṛiṣhṇasya muktasaṅgaḥ paraṁ vrajet
(Shreemad Bhagavatam 12.3.51)

This verse from the Shreemad Bhagavatam states that *Kaliyug*, the present era, is an ocean of faults—people have disturbed minds, unsound health, they live in polluted environment, and face disturbing situations. However, there is one very great virtue in *Kaliyug*. By lovingly chanting the melodious *Kīrtans* of the Lord, one can easily get liberated from material bondage.

The Daily Routine

The best time for doing *Bhakti* is in the morning. When you wake up, your mind is vacant. It is easy to focus it on Radha Krishna. Also, in the morning, the atmosphere is fresh and calm, making it conducive for elevating the mind. However, it is not compulsory to do the devotional practice only in the morning. If your morning is busy with other engagements, then do your daily devotion in the afternoon, evening, or night, depending upon your convenience. But try to make it a rule to stick to the same time every day. This will help in disciplining the mind.

How much time should we spend on devotion? The ideal would be to do it for one hour every day. We spend twenty-four hours a day taking care of the body and its desires. Let us keep this one hour for the soul.

A suggested sequence of what to do for the one hour, is given below:

1. Preparation

Clean the altar. With great reverence, wipe the pictures or deities with a cloth. If you have fresh garlands or flowers, offer them to the picture deities. Else, place bead garlands around them. Light incense sticks, offer their aroma to the picture deities, and place them on the stand.

2. Daily Prayer (5 minutes)

Sit before the altar with folded hands. Say the daily prayer with great sincerity. This prayer is in the Bal-Mukund Wisdom Book.

3. Meditation (15 minutes)

Meditate on your Beloved Radha Krishna and your Gurudev for 15 minutes, as explained in the next chapter.

4. *Kīrtan* (30 minutes)

From the Bal-Mukund Wisdom book, select the *kīrtans* and verses of your choice and sing them melodiously. You will benefit most if you do it with deep feeling, and strong faith that God and His Names are non-different. To ensure that your mind does not waver, visualize the presence of Radha Krishna and Gurudev before you, as you sing.

5. *Bhog* offering (5 minutes)

Place some tasteful food or fruits on a plate, and put the plate on the altar. Pray to Radha Krishna to accept your humble offering. For Their pleasure, you can sing the beautiful *bhog*

song in the Bal-Mukund Wisdom Book.

6. ***Ārati*** (5 minutes)

Let everyone present stand up for the *ārati*. Light the lamp in the *ārati* plate. Do the *ārati*, first of your Guru, and then of Radha Krishna, by taking the *ārati* lamp in big circles around the picture deities. It will be very enjoyable if you sing the *āratis* from the Wisdom Book alongside.

7. Conclusion

Take the *ārati* plate around. People can receive Blessings by placing their hands on the flame, and then putting it on their heads and eyes. Distribute the *prasād*, or the remnants of the food that God has eaten.

Chapter 18 The Art of Meditation

The Benefits of Concentration

At present, our mind is unfocussed. This scattering of the mind in various directions, not only reduces our effectiveness at work, it also becomes an impediment in devotion. We experience that when we sit to chant verses praising God, the mind wanders in the world. Meditation is a process for practicing to focus the mind.

The untrained mind has been compared with a monkey. By nature, a monkey is restless. In addition, if it also has hysteria, how restless will it become? On top of that, if you make it drink alcohol, then consider its state. Further, if you tie a scorpion to its tail, then imagine the monkey's condition. The Saint Tulsidas said, "My Lord! My mind is like such a monkey." He said it out of humility, but we all experience that the mind does wander beyond our control. This negatively impacts our performance at every task.

Concentration increases the effectiveness. Water vapor rises from lakes, and drifts ineffectively in the sky. But the same water vapor, when concentrated in the form of steam and focused on the piston of the railway engine, becomes so powerful that it is able to push the engine on the railway track, along with thousands of tons of carriages, at the speed of hundreds of miles per hour. Similarly, an unwavering mind has tremendous power. This is the reason why peoples in diverse cultures around the world use a variety of meditational techniques to improve their concentration.

Various techniques of Meditation

People practice meditation in many ways. Some meditate on the breath, others on the centre of the eyebrows, yet others on the psychic centers in the spinal cord, still others on a tranquil lake, and while some meditate on a light. These different meditations do improve the focus of the mind. However, their benefits are incomplete and impermanent.

The problem with these mechanical techniques is that they do not address the issue of purification of the mind. As long as lust, anger, greed, envy, illusion, etc. reside in the mind, these forces again destroy the gained concentration.

The second problem is that they aim at stopping the thought flow and bringing the mind to a void. This is against the nature of the mind, and hence these techniques are uninteresting and difficult.

Advantages of Meditating upon God

Let us say, you are riding a bicycle. If you apply the brakes, you will not be able to retain your balance. You will either fall to the left or to the right. However, if you turn the handle, the cycle will turn very easily in the direction you want. Similarly, the mind is such a machine that continuously generates thoughts.

If you want it to stop thinking, it becomes an unstable condition. Such a thoughtless state is difficult to sustain. However, if you turn the mind towards God, it very easily begins meditating upon the Divine Realm.

Meditation upon God is also very sweet. The mind by nature, desires attractive forms, activities, sounds, smells, sensations, tastes, etc. In devotion, the all-Blissful Forms of God are attractive subject matters for the mind to meditate upon.

Most importantly, God is all-pure, and when we fix our mind upon Him, the mind too becomes pure. The Bhagavad Geeta states:

मां च योऽव्यभिचारेण भक्तियोगेन सेवते।
स गुणान्समतीत्यैतान्ब्रह्मभूयाय कल्पते।। (भगवद् गीता १४.२६)

mām̐ cha yo 'vyabhichāreṇa bhaktiyogena sevate
sa guṇānsamatītyaitānbrahmabhūyāya kalpate
(Bhagavad Geeta 14.26)

Shree Krishna tells Arjun: "I am beyond the three modes of material nature. By engaging the mind in meditation upon Me, through *Bhakti yog*, your mind will transcend the three modes and become Divine."

Roop Dhyān

Roop Dhyān is meditation upon the Form of God. In this, we learn to close our eyes, and visualize the Form of God in front of us, or within our heart. Since the Form of God is all-attractive, the mind gets a wonderful subject on which to focus. In this way, the mind stabilizes with loving thoughts upon God.

You may ask that when you have never seen Radha Krishna,

then how can you bring Their Forms to your mind? However, God is so merciful that He says you can make His Form as you wish.

If you are attracted to beautiful Deities of Radha Krishna in some temple, you can make Them the basis of your meditation. Carefully look at Them with your eyes open. Then close your eyes and try bringing Their image in front of you. Else, you can meditate on a nice picture of Radha Krishna. Or you may simply make Their image with your mind. In whatever way you meditate upon Their form, try to feel Their Divine presence in it, and increase your love for Them.

If you wish, you may meditate on Shree Krishna alone, or on Radharani alone. Else you can bring the image of both of Them to your mind; that is all up to you. Some people like to meditate on their Guru alone. That is fine too. The idea is to keep the mind in the Divine Realm. The best is to first meditate on your Guru, to receive his blessings, then meditate upon God.

Meditating upon Divine Virtues

Our mind is also attracted to people's qualities. We say, "This person is so kind-hearted." "This woman is so gentle." "This boy is so intelligent." "This girl is so honest." In this way, our mind's nature is to dwell upon people's qualities. We can do the same in devotion too. We can bring the unlimited Divine qualities of Radha Krishna to our mind.

With the image of Radha Krishna in front of you, think of Their Divine virtues: "They are an ocean of mercy." "They possess unlimited Divine Knowledge." "They are so calm and contented." "They are the veritable form of Love." "They are so beautiful." Meditate upon these virtues in God and Guru. And then, visualize these qualities flowing from Them to you.

In this way, feel yourself becoming calm, peaceful, contented, knowledgeable, generous, loving, etc. Similarly, perceive the Grace of God flowing into your mind and body.

Meditating upon Divine Pastimes

You can further absorb your mind in Radha Krishna by meditating upon Their Divine *leelas*. For example, think that They are coming to your house, and you are welcoming Them

with great love and respect. You can serve Them in various ways. Wash Their feet, perform Their *ārati*, offer Them food, etc., all in your meditation itself. This is called *mānasī sevā*, or serving the Lord in the mind. It will rapidly increase your love for God.

If you wish to be more playful, you can even visualize yourself playing games like cricket, baseball, and tennis with the Lord! In this manner, you can increase your love for Him. The fact is that God has unlimited pastimes. Each time He takes an Avatar, He displays different pastimes. And He has taken unlimited Avatars since eternity. The scriptures state:

नाना भाँति राम अवतारा। रामायन सत कोटि अपारा।। (रामायण)

nānā bhāñti rāma avatārā, rāmāyana sata koṭi apārā (Ramayan)

हरि अनन्त हरि कथा अनन्ता।। (रामायण)

hari ananta hari kathā anantā (Ramayan)

The above verses state that Lord Ram descended in the material world innumerable times in countless ages. Each time He performed different pastimes. Hence, there are innumerable Ramayans in existence. God is unlimited, and His Pastimes are also unlimited. These infinite pastimes include the *leelas* we meditate upon in our mind. Besides, in the Divine Abodes of God, He keeps engaging in ever-new *leelas* at every moment. Hence, you have the freedom to imagine the *leelas* of God as you wish.

God's Divine Abode

In this material realm, we are all under the bondage of Maya, and we are transmigrating in different bodies, from life to life.

In each life, we experience birth, disease, old-age, and death. We will continue doing so in future lives, until are released from Maya. This material world is like a prison house, where we souls have been put since we have turned our backs towards God. However, the moment we attain God, this Maya will release us and we will not have to take birth in this world again. Where will the soul go to after that?

The Vedas state that beyond this material realm is the Divine abode of God:

न तत्र सूर्यो भाति न चन्द्रतारकं
नेमा विद्युतो भान्ति कुतोऽयमग्निः। (कठ उपनिषद् २.२.१५)

na tatra sūryo bhāti na chandratārakaṁ
nemā vidyuto bhānti kuto 'yamagniḥ
(Kaṭha Upanishad 2.2.15)

"Where the sun, moon, stars, light, and fire of this universe cannot go. That place is the Divine abode of God." The Bhagavad Geeta states:

न तद्भासयते सूर्यो न शशाङ्को न पावकः।
यद्गत्वा न निवर्तन्ते तद्धाम परमं मम।। (भगवद् गीता १५.६)

na tadbhāsayate sūryo na śhaśhāṅko na pāvakaḥ
yadgatvā na nivartante taddhāma paramaṁ mama
(Bhagavad Geeta 15.6)

Shree Krishna says: "That place, which is beyond the light of the sun and the moon; where having gone once, a person does not come back to the material realm; that is My Divine abode."

According to the Vedas and the Bhagavad Geeta, this material realm is only one-fourth of creation. The other three-fourths is the Divine creation. In that Divine realm, there are many abodes. Each Form of God has His own abode. Vaikunth Lok is the abode of Narayan. Saket Lok is the abode of Lord Ram, and Golok is the abode of Lord Krishna.

In these abodes, God performs Divine pastimes with liberated souls who reside there. When we become God-realized, we too will go to His Divine abode, and in a divine body, we will participate in God's pastimes. If we wish, even now, in our mind, we can meditate on the Divine Abode of God.

Increase Your Longing to Meet Shree Krishna

In this way, when we meditate on the Names, Forms, Virtues, Pastimes, Abodes, and Devotees of God, our mind will progressively become pure. Consequently, our longing for meeting Radha Krishna will increase. This will purify the mind even further. And that will increase the longing even more. Finally, when the mind is totally cleansed, by the Grace of God and our Guru, we will receive Divine Love for God.

When we are bestowed with that Divine power, the bondage of Maya will cease. We will be given God's unlimited Divine Bliss and Knowledge. Even while we remain in this body, we will be in a liberated state. When we leave our body at the end of our life, we will go the Divine abode of God, and in a Divine body, we will serve Him in His eternal pastimes.卐

Jagadguru Shree Kripaluji Maharaj

A Brief Introduction

Eternally liberated Divine personalities sometimes descend upon the earth for the welfare of humankind. Jagadguru Shree Kripaluji Maharaj is such a Divine personality. "Maharajji", as he is lovingly called by his devotees, was born on the auspicious night of Sharat Poornima in 1922, in the village Mangarh, near Allahabad.

Childhood and Youth

He spent his childhood excelling effortlessly in his studies. Then at the age of fourteen, he left his village and attended three Universities, in Kashi, Chitrakoot, and Indore. There he covered a whole series of courses in the space of just two-and-a-half years.

Absorbtion in Divine *Samādhi*

At the young age of sixteen, he suddenly gave up his studies and entered the dense forests of Chitrakoot. There he spent his time absorbed in intense love for Radha Krishna. Often he would lose all external consciousness, and go without eating and drinking for many days at a stretch. For long intervals, he would remain in *Mahābhāv*, the highest stage of devotion that manifests in Radharani. These symptoms of *Mahābhāv* love had also manifested in Chaitanya Mahaprabhu, 500 years ago. He emerged from the forest after two years to begin his mission of revealing the glories of Radha Krishna devotion to the world.

Devotional Literature

Kripaluji Maharaj has written thousands of verses revealing the Divine pastimes of Radha Krishna. His style of writing is unique: he begins the chanting of a *pada* or *kīrtan*, and then keeps adding lines to it, as it goes along.

Kīrtan Movement

He then started conducting *satsaṅgs* that brought about a flood of *Bhakti* in the states of UP and Rajasthan in the 1940s and 50s. He would lead *kīrtans* imbued with intense devotion, which would continue throughout the night. These *kīrtans*, which he wrote himself, have been compared by scholars with those of Meerabai, Soordas, Tulsidas, and Ras Khan.

Jagadguruttam

In the past 5000 years of the present age of *Kali*, five personalities have been recognized as original *Jagadgurus*: Jagadguru Shankaracharya, Jagadguru Nimbarkacharya, Jagadguru Ramanujacharya, and Jagadguru Madhvacharya.

In January 1957, Shree Kripalu ji Maharaj gave a profound series of lectures at the invitation of the *Kāśhī Vidvat Pariṣhat*, a body of 500 of the topmost Vedic scholars of India who collectively represent the seat of spiritual learning. With profound admiration, the scholars accepted that his knowledge was deeper than the combined knowledge of all 500 of them put together. They unanimously acclaimed him as *Jagadguru*, the Spiritual Master of the world. They further added that he was "Jagadguruttam," or Supreme amongst all *Jagadgurus*.

Scriptural Discourses

After accepting the title of *Jagadguru*, Kripaluji Maharaj travelled throughout the country for fourteen years. He would deliver month-long discourses in each city, in which he would unravel the mysteries of the scriptures before the public. Tens of thousands of people would throng to these discourses, and listen spellbound while he tantalized them with humour, worldly examples, pratical instructions, and chastisement. It was a unique experience as he made the deepest scriptural truths accessible to everyone in the simplest language.

Worldwide Mission

To enable the worldwide spread of his teachings, Kripaluji Maharaj began training preachers and sending them to different parts of the globe. He also created a formal organization and began the construction of huge *āśhrams*, to provide facilities for devotees who wished to practically apply the teachings in their lives. This organization is today known as the Jagadguru Kripalu Parishat, and it oversees the worldwide mission of Maharajji. Its sister organizations are Jagadguru Kripalu Yog Trust in India, Jagadguru Kripaluji Yog in USA, and Radha Govind Dham in various cities around the world.

(For more information, please visit www.jkyog.org)

Glossary

A

Āchārya—Spiritual teacher who is thorough with the knowledge of the scriptures.

Agni Dev—The celestial god of fire.

Ānand—The Bliss of God.

Apar dharm—The social aspect of religion, including duties towards parents, friends and relatives, the society we live in, and the nation whose citizens we are, etc.

Ārati—Ceremony of lights, in which, with great faith and reverence, a lamp is waved around the deity or image of God.

Āsan/Yogāsan—Yogic exercise or posture for health and wellbeing.

Āśhram—Place similar to a monastery where dedicated spiritual practitioners reside.

Aṣhṭāṅg Yog—The eight-fold process of Yog described by Sage Patanjali.

Ātmā—The real self, or "soul", that is spiritual in nature, and which imparts consciousness to the body.

Ātmagyān—Knowledge of the self or soul.

Avatar—The descension of God in His personal form, on the earth planet.

B

Bhagavad Geeta—A popular Vedic scriptures. The name literally means "Song of God". It contains the dialogue between Shree Krishna and Arjun on the battlefield of Kurukshetra, in 700 verses.

Bhagavān—The Supreme Lord. The word is also used to refer to His personal form, distinct from His other aspects.

Bhakti—Devotion.

Bhaktiyog—The path of attaining God through *Bhakti*.

Bhāv—A sentiment kept towards God as a part of devotion.

Bhog—Food that is especially placed on a plate to be offered to God. After the offering, it is accepted as *prasād*, or the Grace of God.

Brahm—The aspect of God that is all-pervading in the world.

Brahma—The first created being in the material universe. Brahma, who is himself born from Lord Vishnu, creates the various life forms and the substance of the world from the material energy.

Brahm Niṣhṭh—One who is situated on the platform of God-realization.

Brahmānand—The Bliss of *Brahm*, the formless all-pervading aspect of God.

Brahmagyān—Knowledge of God.

Braj—The land in the district of Mathura, India, where Shree Krishna performed His childhood pastimes 5000 years ago. It includes many holy places like Vrindaban, Goverdhan, Barsana, Nandagaaon, and Gokul.

C

Chit—Sentient, possessing knowledge.

D

Darśhan—Philosophic text written by a sage.

Devatā—Celestial god who governs some particular affairs of the material world from the higher abodes.

Dharm—The set of duties described by the scriptures, which are a part of religious behavior.

G

Gadā—Mace.

Ganga—A holy river that begins at the feet of Shree Vishnu and descends from the celestial abodes, to flow in India. It is also spelt as Ganges in English.

Ghee—Clarified butter.

Golok—The Divine abode of Shree Krishna, which exists in the spiritual realm, beyond this material world.

Gopīs—The village maidens who resided in Braj when Shree Krishna manifested His *leelas* 5000 years ago.

Guru—A God-realized teacher of spirituality who illumines people with the knowledge of God.

Gyān—Knowledge.

Gyān yog—The path of knowing the "self" through the practice of knowledge.

Gyānī—One who follows the path of *Gyān yog*.

I

Indra Dev—The king of heaven, who is the celestial god of rain.

Itihās—These are the two historical texts of the Indian Civilization, Ramayan and Mahabharat.

J

Jagadguru—Spiritual Master of the world; similar to the Pope in Christianity.

Ji—Suffix added after someone's name as a mark of respect.

K

Kailash—The Abode of Lord Shankar within this material realm.

Kaliyug—The present era on the earth planet. This was preceded by *Dvāparyug, Tretāyug,* and *Satyug.*

Karm—Work in accordance with the prescribed rules of the Vedas.

Karm Yog—The path of attaining God while doing one's Karm.

Karma—Action performed by an individual, of which God keeps an account.

Karmakāṇḍ—Ritualistic ceremonies that help purify the mind and control the senses.

Kāśhī Vidvat Pariṣhat—The supreme body of Vedic scholars in the city of Kashi (highest seat of Vedic learning).

Kīrtan—The singing of the Names, Virtues, and Pastimes of God, usually done in a group.

Kriyamāṇ—The karmas one performs in the present by exercise of one's free will.

Kuber—The celestial god of wealth.

L

Leela—A Divine pastime enacted by God in His personal form.

M

Mahabharat—A 100,000 verse-long poem written by Ved Vyas describing the history of India in *Dvāparyug*, with emphasis on the pastimes of Shree Krishna.

Maharṣhi—A great Sage.

Mānasī Sevā—Visualizing and serving the form of God in one's mind.

Mantra—Sacred hymn written in Sanskrit.

Maya—The material energy from which this world is created. It also puts souls, who are forgetful of God, into illusion, and makes them transmigrate in the cycle of life and death.

O

Oṁ Namaḥ Shivaya—A popular phrase chanted by the devotees of Lord Shiv, literally meaning, "I offer my obeisance to Lord Shiv."

P

Pada—Devotinal song.

Par Dharm—The spiritual aspect of religion, i.e. devotion towards God.

Paramātmā—The aspect of God that resides in the hearts of all living beings.

Prārabdh—The destiny one is allotted at the time of birth, based on past karmas.

Prakṛiti—The original form of the material energy, which unwinds at the time of creation to manifest the world.

Prasād—After food offering is made to God, the remnants are considered Prasād, or the Grace of God.

Premānand—The Bliss of Bhagavān, the personal form of God.

Pūjā—Worship ceremony, act of worshipping.

Purāṇas—These are scriptures, full of philosophic knowledge, that discuss the creation of the universe, its annihilation and recreation, the history of humankind etc. There are eighteen *Puraṇas*, all written by Ved Vyas.

Purușhārth—The self-effort one does in the present with the exercise of one's free will, as distinct from destiny.

R

Rāgas—Standardized musical compositions in Indian classical music.

Rajo guṇa—The mode of passion; one of the three modes of material nature.

Rājasic—Having the quality of *rajoguṇa*.

Ramayan—The historical description of the pastimes of Lord Ram, originally written by Sage Valmiki.

Roop Dhyān—Meditation upon the Form of God.

S

Sādhanā—Spiritual practice.

Sādhan Bhakti—Preparatory devotion, which is done to cleanse the heart and prepare it for receiving *Siddha Bhakti*.

Saket Lok—The Divine abode of Shree Ram, which exists in the spiritual realm, beyond this material world.

Samādhi—State of trance attained when the mind is in complete absorption on God or the self.

Sanātan—Eternal.

Sanātan Dharm—Eternal religion. This is the name of the religion described in the Vedas. The word Hinduism was coined much later.

Sañchit Karma—All the accumulated karmas of the soul in endless past lifetimes.

Sanyāsī—A person in the renounced order of life.

Sarva-śhaktimān—The all-powerful God.

Sat—That which is eternal.

Satsaṅg—A congregation in which the Names, Virtues, and Pastimes of God are sung and remembered.

Sattva guṇa—The mode of goodness; one of the three modes of material nature.

Sāttvic—Having the quality of *sattva guṇa*.

Śhakti—Energy or power.

Shiv Liṅg—The symbol for Lord Shiv that is worshipped in temples. It is usually made of stone and is shaped like a pillar.

Shreemad Bhagavatam—The most important of the eighteen *Purāṇas* written by Ved Vyas. It consists of 18,000 verses, full of philosophical knowledge and the descriptions of the Names, Forms, Virtues, and Pastimes of the various Avatars of God.

Śhrotriya—A person who is well-versed in the theoretical knowledge of the scriptures.

Śhruti—Another name for the Vedas. It means knowledge that was passed down by the tradition of hearing from master to disciple.

Siddha Bhakti—Divine Love or perfect devotion, which is a power of God, and is received by His Grace.

Smṛiti—Knowledge that was revealed in the heart of sages, who then put it down in writing as scriptures.

Sumeru Mountain—A famous mountain in the celestial abode.

Swarg—The higher abodes within the material world, which have far greater facility for enjoyment than the earth planet, but are not beyond the cycle of life and death.

T

Tāmasic—Having the quality of *tamoguṇa.*

Tamo guṇa—The mode of ignorance; one of the three modes of material nature.

Tāṇḍav—The dance performed by Lord Shiv with which He annihilates the world at the time of dissolution.

Tānpurā—Indian musical stringed instrument.

Tridhā Bhakti—Three-fold devotion consisting of singing, hearing, and remembering.

U

Upanishads—These are philosophical texts that constitute a section of the Vedas.

Upāsanā—Devotion.

V

Vaikunth—The Divine abode of Lord Vishnu in the spiritual realm, beyond the material world.

Varṇāśhram—The social system, in which one's duties were defined according to one's occupation and stage in life.

Varuṇa Dev— The celestial god of the ocean.

Vāyu Dev—The celestial god of the wind.

Vedas—The eternal knowledge of God that He manifested at the beginning of creation, and which was passed down from master to disciple through hearing, and finally divided and written in four books—*Ṛig Veda*, *Yajur Veda*, *Sāma Veda*, and *Atharva Veda*.

Vishnudoots—The servants of Lord Vishnu.

Y

Yamdoots—The servants of Yamraj, who come to take sinful souls after death, to their next destination.

Yamraj—The celestial god of death.

Yagya—Fire sacrifice ritual conducted in accordance with Vedic rules, accompanied by the chanting of mantras and the offering of oblations.

Yogamāyā—The Divine spiritual power of God.

Yogī—One who practices Yog.

Yug Dharma—The spiritual practice most suitable to the present era.

Other Publications by Jagadguru Kripaluji Yog

1. Yoga for the Body, Mind, and Soul
2. Spiritual Dialectics
3. Inspiring stories for Children Volume 1
4. Inspiring Stories for Children Volume 2
5. Inspiring Stories for Children Volume 3
6. Inspiring Stories for Children Volume 4
7. Saints of India
8. Festivals of India
9. Healthy Body Healthy Mind – Yoga for Children
10. Bal-Mukund Wisdom Book
11. Bal-Mukund Painting Book